Joseph L. Lord

Briefs on Prophetic Themes

Joseph L. Lord

Briefs on Prophetic Themes

ISBN/EAN: 9783337067878

Printed in Europe, USA, Canada, Australia, Japan

Cover: Foto ©Lupo / pixelio.de

More available books at **www.hansebooks.com**

BRIEFS

ON

PROPHETIC THEMES.

BY A MEMBER OF THE BOSTON BAR.

"Return for thy servants' sake, the tribes of thine inheritance. The people of thy holiness have possessed it but a little while: our adversaries have trodden down thy sanctuary. We are thine: thou never barest rule over them; they were not called by thy name."—ISAIAH lxiii. 17—19.

"Speak ye comfortably to Jerusalem, and cry unto her, that her warfare is accomplished, that her iniquity is pardoned: for she hath received of the Lord's hand double for all her sins."—ISAIAH xl. 2.

BOSTON:
E. P. DUTTON & COMPANY.
NEW YORK: HURD & HOUGHTON.
1864.

Entered according to Act of Congress, in the year 1864,
By E. P. DUTTON & Co.,
in the Clerk's Office of the District Court of the District of Massachusetts.

BOSTON:
PRINTED BY AUG. A. KINGMAN,
116, Washington Street.

I inscribe these pages to my children, too young as yet to fully apprehend their meaning, in the hope that, in after life, their appeal, in all moral issues, some of which are herein indicated, may be, ever and only, to the Word and providence of their heavenly Father, and to the guidance of his Holy Spirit.

PREFACE.

We were led to write the following pages by a perusal of some of the writings of Doctors S. P. Tregelles and B. W. Newton, of Plymouth, England. Some of their views, though harmonizing with views we had previously entertained, were new to us. These, upon consideration, we have adopted, and now reproduce. Other views, as well as our method of treatment, are our own, for which these most learned and estimable Bible scholars, to whom we have been so deeply indebted, can, in no sense, be held responsible.

THE AUTHOR.

Boston, November, 1864.

CONTENTS.

	Page
PREFACE.	4

THE PROPHETIC EARTH OF DANIEL AND THE REVELATION. Scripture symbols of the rise, decline, and fall, of the four great Gentile Powers. 9

THE LITERAL BABYLON OF PROPHECY. Its final destruction co-incident with the future restoration of Israel. . . 22

THE SYMBOLIC BABYLON OF PROPHECY. Its composite character, including, not Romanism only, but all forms of false religion and infidelity. 38

THE ANTICHRIST OF PROPHECY. The restoration of the Jews in unbelief, and their subsequent persecution by Antichrist. . . . . , 58

ISRAEL AND JERUSALEM OF PROPHECY. God's covenants concerning them, and their final exaltation. . . 80

APPENDIX. Extracts from Colonel Chesney's Report, etc. 105

CHAPTER I.

THE PROPHETIC EARTH OF DANIEL AND THE REVELATION.

DATING from the palmiest hours of Babylonian greatness, under Nebuchadnezzar, and the co-incident decline and fall of the Jewish Theocracy, it will not be denied that the four great empires of Babylon, Persia, Greece and Rome have figured more conspicuously than any other Gentile powers in the world's history; nor that they have a distinctly recognized historic existence in the prophetic Scriptures; nor, whatever allusions may therein be made to other powers, that such allusions are merely incidental, revealing no specific outline, nor any approach to an outline, of their history, as of the history of the four empires thus made the special subjects of prophetic mention. The reasons of this election are hidden in the counsels of the Divine Mind. The fact that such discrimination exists, that such an election is actually made, is alone pertinent to our present purpose.

The dreams of Nebuchadnezzar and the visions of Daniel embrace the whole period of Gentile civilization, from the conquest, by Nebuchadnezzar, of the two tribes of Judah and Benjamin—the ten revolted tribes of Israel having, long before, been lost in their still mysterious and impenetrable captivity—down to the *closing scenes of the present dispensation.* These dreams and visions, interpreted, the former by Daniel, and the latter by direct angelic agency, together with the visions of the apostle of Patmos, as recorded in the Revelation (which latter visions unveil those *closing scenes,* with respect to the *specific instrumentalities* by which they will be accomplished), have a marked geographical import, and relate, exclusively, to those portions of the earth which were contained within the territorial limits of these four empires, more especially the Roman, as embracing within its boundaries a larger portion of the earth's surface than either of its predecessors, and as being the subject of more minute and extended prophetic detail.

Wherefore it is that, in a distinctive sense, we term the territory thus incorporated, *the prophetic earth.*

This distinctive appellation will be found to be fully justified upon careful reference to the two great apocalyptic writers of the Old and New Testaments, the book of Daniel being not less the Apocalypse of the Old Testament, than the book of the Revelation the Apocalypse of the New, the former forecasting the whole future of the four empires, the latter, in its relation to the closing scenes of this dispensation, confining itself chiefly to the Roman.

Hence we style the prophetic earth, as thus indicated, *the prophetic earth of Daniel and the Revelation.*

The second chapter of Daniel, under the symbol of an inanimate image, presents an outline of the secular history of these empires, in respect to both the *intrinsic* and *comparative value* of *governmental power,* as severally and successively exercised by them. The seventh chapter, under the symbol of four fierce and devouring beasts, presents an outline of their several histories, in respect to the *moral quality* of the *practical use* and *exercise* of that power. Neither chapter, however, gives any account of their territorial or chronological boundaries. These are clearly determinable from profane history. The dignity of the inspired record stoops not thus to justify itself, or to confirm its never-to-be-questioned verity.

The wondrous Image of Daniel ii. 31—46, glorious and terrible, looking, as with lordly supremacy, down the dim vista of the coming ages, to the very end of the present Gentile dispensation, comprehends, with careful precision, the prophetic earth as we have defined it, but has no direct, nor any thing more than a merely influential, application to other regions of the earth. This distinction it is of great importance to note.

The prophet Daniel, in revealing and interpreting to Nebuchadnezzar the dream of the Image, assured him that *his* kingdom, or the empire of Babylon, was its *head*. "Thou art this head of gold." Its head was not of silver, or of brass, or of iron, or of gold even of any uncertain quality. "The Image's head was of *fine* gold." Now, therefore, as gold is the most precious of metals, and as *fineness* is the term used to designate its highest value, it follows that the golden head of the Image must be a symbol, in some special and distinctive sense, be that sense what it may, of *governmental power*, in, intrinsically, its most precious form.

But what *is* the special sense thus indicated? To answer this question, we need but to inquire, what single and surpassing attribute, if any, of governmental power, most distinguished the empire of Babylon, and contributed most largely to make it preëminent over the three empires that succeeded it? To this inquiry but one answer can be given, which is, that no attribute so distinguished either its own exaltation, or its preëminence over its successors, as its absolute autocracy and royalty of power. The prophet said to Nebuchadnezzar; "Thou, O king, art a king of kings, for the God of heaven hath given thee a kingdom, power, and strength, and glory; and wheresoever the children of men dwell, the beasts of the field, and the fowls of heaven, hath he given into thine hand, and hath made thee ruler over them all." * So also in Jeremiah xxvii. 5, 6: "Thus saith the Lord of Hosts, the God of Israel; Thus shall ye say unto your masters; I have made the earth, the man and the beast that are upon the ground, by my great power and by my outstretched arm, and have given it unto whom it seemed meet unto me. And now I have given all these lands into the hand of Nebuchadnezzar the king of Babylon, my servant; and the beasts of the field have I given him also to serve him."

Truly, a grant of power scarcely less absolute and un-

---

* Dr. Tregelles, in commenting upon this passage, has well observed; "These words do not imply that Nebuchadnezzar actually held and exercised this rule over every part of the inhabited earth; but rather that, so far as God was concerned, all was given into his hand; so that he was not limited as to the power which he might obtain, in whatever direction he might turn himself as conqueror; the only earthly bound to his empire was his own ambition." Tregelles' Daniel, p. 7.

So also Newton; "This gift was granted to Nebuchadnezzar in consequence of his being part of the Image, and was not dependent upon his power being "golden" in character. The endowment of all the successive empires was similar to his. Hence their assumption of names or expressions implying universality of dominion; and their title to do this is sanctioned in Scripture. The Romans were accustomed to call their empire "Orbis Terrarum," and in Scripture the corresponding expression πᾶσα ἡ οἰκουμένη, is used. "There went out a decree from Cæsar Augustus that the *whole world* (πᾶσα ἡ οἰκουμένη,) should be taxed." Thus also Cyrus says, "the God of Heaven hath given me all the kingdoms of the earth." Ezra i. 2.

limited in its terms than that conferred upon Adam before his fall. With how sublime a title, with what glorious privileges, Gentile civilization set forth upon its career! How deserved its predicted doom, if recreant to so godlike a trust!

The head of gold could not have been a symbol of this empire, in respect to the extent of its *territorial* dominion, for, in this respect, it was inferior to each of the empires symbolised by silver, and brass, and iron, that succeeded it. To what, therefore, can the " fine gold" refer, but to governmental power in the supremest form in which it was ever conferred upon a Gentile king?

Assuming, then — with all history, sacred and profane, for our warrant — that the kingdom of Nebuchadnezzar, as thus symbolised, was sovereign power in its most unrestrained, its most autocratic, its most nearly theocratic, sense, the symbol further teaches that this form of power is, in itself, not only precious, but the most precious, and that it is, or can be, evil, and was evil in the case of Nebuchadnezzar, in its *misuse* or *maladministration* only. If it were evil in itself, it would not have been conferred upon Nebuchadnezzar, as we have seen that it was, by the direct gift of the Almighty, nor could it be conferred by the Almighty, as we know that it will be, upon Him, of whom, in prophetic vision, it is said, " The sovereignty of the world has become the sovereignty of our God and of his Christ, and He shall reign for ever and ever."

"After thee shall arise another kingdom inferior to thee "—" the breast and arms of *silver*." This kingdom is admitted, by the common consent of all expositors, to be the immediate successor of the Babylonian, to wit, the

Medo-Persian. The arms have been supposed to represent, the one Media, and the other Persia. This seems probable enough, but is not material to our purpose. This empire was not, like its predecessor, an absolute monarchy, but a limited sovereignty. It was, as appears both from Scripture and profane history, an *aristocratic monarchy*, the nobles, or men of birth, being, not the supporters only, but, in an important sense, controllers of the crown, and in all respects, save official rank, its equals. The extent of their influence is shown in the decree which consigned Daniel to the den of lions. Not so did Nebuchadnezzar rule. In his *golden* power, he would have consigned such counsellors to the den themselves, rather than forego the exercise of his royal will, for " whom he would he slew, and whom he would he kept alive." So, also, the Persian monarch, Ahasuerus (in the book of Esther), and his princes *acted together*, and the king could not undo what they had *jointly decreed* concerning Queen Vashti. And in Ezra vii. 14, we find authority given to that servant of God *from the king and his seven counsellors*. All this shows, not a king acting in right of his royal prerogative, but controlled by counsellors, *without whose advice and consent he could not act*. Power was beginning to lose its golden excellence, precisely as the metals symbolising it were beginning to lessen, not in value only, but, it will be noticed, in specific gravity also; thus exhibiting the reverse of stability as we descend the Image. Circumstances arose, with which the depreciated power of the monarchs of Persia soon found itself unable to contend.

That silver was the symbol of both the intrinsic and relative value of the Persian form of governmental power, and not of the territorial extent of its dominion, is evident, because, in military prowess and extent of territorial acquisition, it was not inferior to the Babylonian. On the contrary, it subjugated, under Cyrus, regions (Asia Minor, for example), which the monarchs of Chaldea never reached, so that, in this respect, it was not only not inferior, but far superior to its predecessor. And this is the aspect under which the vision of the Image continually presents itself. It is a symbolic outline of the history of the four great Gentile empires, in respect to the character of their power.

Next succeeded the Greek or Greco-Macedonian empire of Alexander—"the belly and thighs of *brass*." The identity of this symbol with this empire is admitted without a question. Alexander, "the great scourge and destroyer of Asia," but of superlative ambition (which the elder Napoleon affected in vain), with his brazen-coated legions, before the close of his brief reign, at the early age of thirty-two years, had far exceeded both the Persian and the Chaldean monarchs, alike in the celerity of his conquests, and the territorial extent of his dominions. Elsewhere in Daniel he is represented under the symbol of a "winged leopard." His conquests extended across Asia Minor, Syria and Egypt, to Affghanistan and the Indus; and he paused not, if we may credit tradition, until compelled to pause, weeping that he had no more worlds to conquer. And yet the character of his power is only worthy of being symbolised by brass, not a precious metal, but a mere alloy. And when, upon his death, his empire was divided between his four victorious generals, whose proud, fierce spirits had been nursed amidst the democracies of southern Greece, it is a fact, most significant of the gradual depreciation of Gentile power, that, at Rome, an ounce of silver was equivalent, according to Gibbon, to about seventy pounds' weight of brass.

The Greco-Macedonian empire was a *military oligarchy*, a still inferior grade of power.

Thus descending the Image, we reach, at last, the empire of the Cæsars — " the legs of *iron*, the feet part of iron and part of *clay*." This empire, in its subdivisions, still, in the prophetic sense, exists, and will continue to exist, until the number of its subdivisions, *East and West together*, shall have reached its full complement, which it has never reached as yet; and until the present Gentile dispensation shall terminate, upon the overthrow, by the " stone cut out of the mountain without hands," of their representative and united strength, before the walls of Jerusalem. This empire, in its earlier development under the Cæsars, is represented by the symbol of unmixed iron. Its completed development, that of the ten sovereignties, European, Asiatic and African, into which it will eventually be subdivided, is represented under the symbol of iron mixed with " miry clay," referring, unquestionably, to the mixed monarchical and popular, or populo-monarchic, character of these ten sovereignties, upon this eventual subdivision of the Roman empire, formed to so large an extent already.

The term " miry," as applied to clay, is not less significant of the relative value of the ten toes of the feet of the Image, considered as a symbol of governmental power, than is the term "fineness" of the relative value of the head. A mournful picture, indeed, of the gradual declension, both of the value and the stability of Gentile power, a sad reversal of the flushed and giddy hopes of our vaunted Gentile progress, and Gentile civilization! But is it, for that reason, any less the revealed word of God? We humbly submit that it is God's Word. How can we any more doubt it, than we can doubt the verity of Nebuchadnezzar's dream, or of Daniel's revelation and interpretation of it?

History, sacred and profane, thus bears witness that the dream, as interpreted by Daniel, has come to pass most strictly and literally hitherto, not less so, indeed, than the vision of the "great tree" in Daniel iv. which was fulfilled in Nebuchadnezzar's lifetime. Why then doubt that it will, any the less strictly and literally, continue to come to pass to the very end? As to the divine inspiration and authenticity of the prophet Daniel, our Saviour himself attests it, with an endorsement of the most incontestable character.

Under the dominion of the Cæsars, we reach the most extended limits of the prophetic earth—of that portion of the earth's territory symbolised by the Image—so that as we proceed, we shall use the terms prophetic and Roman earth in an interchangeable sense. The Roman empire, or "*orbis terrarum*" of the Romans, not only, for the most part, included, but, with only here and there an exception, far exceeded the utmost boundaries of the three preceding empires. We can call the countries included in it all by name, whether in the language of ancient or modern geography. We propose to show, in another chapter, that the Roman earth, divided yet united, consisting of ten independent yet confederated kingdoms, will be the special and restricted sphere of the dominion of the last great monarch of the Gentiles, THE ANTICHRIST OF PROPHECY.

The seventh chapter of Daniel represents these four great world powers in respect to the moral quality of the *practical use* or *exercise of* their governmental power, under the symbol, as we have already stated, of four fierce and devouring beasts; the Babylonian being represented by the majestic fulness and preëminence of power of the lion; the Persian by the sullen fierceness and voracity ("devouring much flesh") of the bear; the Greek by the swiftness, and grace, and beauty, but subtilty and malignity of the leopard; the Roman by the stern, and haughty, and crushing strength of a nameless, complicated, ten-horned monster, of indescribable horror, "strong exceedingly," who, in the "last days," under the symbol of a "little horn," "exalting himself above all that is called God or that is worshipped," and representing the consummated glory of Gentile civilization, "shall stand up against the Prince of princes," the Messiah of Israel, to receive from Him his everlasting condemnation.

We question not; on the contrary, we appreciate, and confess ourselves by no means insensible to, the fascinations, the bewildering allurements, the æsthetic refinements, the magnificent attainments of science and of art, the lofty material splendor, of that consummated Gentile glory, which will seem as fair and desirable to the eye and heart of unregenerate man, as the grapes of Sodom or clusters of Gomorrah, but which will not, for that reason, in its general spirit, be any the less hostile to God, or bear any the less the dark impress of Sodom, or hasten with less accelerated speed to the same fearful doom. If it leans on Sodom, with Sodom it must fall.

Witness, finally, the crisis of the Image, the tragical conclusion of Gentile ascendancy:

"A stone was cut out without hands, which smote the image upon its feet that were of iron and clay, and brake them to pieces. Then was the iron, the clay, the brass, the silver and the gold, broken to pieces together, and became like the chaff of the summer threshing floor; and the wind carried them away, that no place was found for them, and the stone that smote the image became a great mountain, and filled the whole earth. . . . . And in the days of these kings [the ten kings, or sovereignties, symbolised by the ten toes of the feet of the image (the two feet referring, not improbably, to the Eastern and Western divisions of the Roman empire), symbolised also, by the ten horns of the fourth beast, or Roman empire—'and the ten horns of this kingdom are the ten kings that shall arise,' Dan. vii. 24] shall the God of heaven set up a kingdom, which shall never be destroyed: and the kingdom shall not be left to other people, but it shall break in pieces and consume all these kingdoms, and it shall stand forever. Forasmuch as thou sawest that the stone was cut out of the mountain without hands, and that it break in pieces the iron, the brass, the clay, the silver and the gold; the great God hath made known to the king what shall come to pass hereafter; and the dream is certain and the interpretation thereof sure."— Daniel ii. 34, 35, 43—45.

Surely, if language is capable of interpreting its own meaning, it is an act, not of peaceful and benignant *blessing*, but of vindictive and destroying *judgment*, that is here described, not the gradual spread and diffusion of the gospel of peace, but the quick, and sudden, and wrathful, and utter destruction of the more than ever proud and stately, but the final and more than ever godless, Babel of Gentile power. "And whosoever shall fall upon this stone shall be broken; but on whomsoever it shall fall, it will grind him to powder."

The "ANCIENT PEOPLE" of God, alone of all the nations of the prophetic earth, will escape the destruction. "IN THOSE DAYS *shall Judah be saved, and Jerusalem shall dwell safely.*"

"And the kingdom and dominion, and the greatness of the kingdom under the whole heaven, shall be given to the people of the saints of the most High, whose kingdom is an everlasting kingdom, and all dominions shall serve and obey him."—Daniel vii. 27.

This verse, as we understand it, describes the glorious sequel of these judicial scenes; the expression, "saints of the most High," referring to the saints, Jew and Gentile, of the present dispensation in their thenceforward risen glory, as inhabitants of the new or heavenly Jerusalem, ministering, as a "royal priesthood" to the blessed inhabitants of earth during its millennial career; and the expression, "people of the saints of the most High," referring to the restored and now forgiven Jewish nation, as the leading nation of the earth during the millennium, dispensing, from the overflowing fulness of its blessings,to all other nations; thus fulfilling the covenant of God with Abraham, and Isaac and Jacob—"and in thy seed shall all the nations of the earth be blessed." *

---

* Dr. Tregelles, in remarking upon this passage, has said; "This appears to me to be a statement, informing us that a certain kingdom, not co-extensive with that of the Son of Man, will be given to a certain nation. Who then can this nation be? Now, it is clear from many Scriptures that Israel will, after they are set in grace, and their blindnesss and consequent rejection are ended, be the head of the nations, and bear rule over the earth. In chapter viii. 24, we find the expression 'the mighty and the holy people,' or, more literally, 'people of the holy ones,' or 'people of the saints,'—this Hebrew phrase answering pretty accurately to the Chaldee used in the passage before us. Now as in chapter viii, the Jews are the nation clearly denoted, so do I consider that they are intended here." Tregelles' Daniel, p. 45.

Have not millennial writers been too much accustomed to dissociate the restored Jewish Theocracy from their conceptions of the millennial kingdom?

CHAPTER II.

THE LITERAL BABYLON OF PROPHECY.

ITS FINAL DESTRUCTION CO-INCIDENT WITH THE FUTURE RESTORATION OF ISRAEL.

PERHAPS no truth is more clearly revealed in prophetic Scripture than the co-incidence of the restoration of both families of the House of Israel, as one nation, to their own land, and the final destruction and desolation of the city and land of Babylon, as predicted by Isaiah and Jeremiah. When the feet of the " outcasts of Israel " and of the " dispersed of Judah " shall stand again within the borders of the " pleasant land," and within the " gates of Jerusalem," then, but not till then, will re-united Israel " take up this parable," and join in this acclaim, " How hath the oppressor ceased—the golden city ceased!" When the whole House of Israel, restored and undivided, shall perform, like any other nation, all the functions of a distinct, organized and recognized nationality in their own land, then, but not till then, will the burden of Babylon, which Isaiah and Jeremiah saw, be fulfilled in her final overthrow. When peace revisits the walls and prosperity the palaces of Jerusalem, when the curse of the Mosaic covenant is revoked, and the blessings of the Abrahamic covenant are ushered in, then, but not till then, will Babylon lie there upon the not distant plains of

Shinar, a sudden and utter wreck, the saddest wreck of all, of Gentile evil greatness and Gentile evil glory.

"Out of the North there cometh up a nation against her [Babylon] which shall make her land desolate, and none shall dwell therein; they shall remove, they shall depart, both man and beast. IN THOSE DAYS, AND IN THAT TIME, saith the Lord, the children of Israel shall come, they and the children of Judah together, going and weeping; they shall go and seek the Lord their God. They shall ask the way to Zion with their faces thitherward, saying, Come let us join ourselves to the Lord in a perpetual covenant that shall not be forgotten."

"Therefore thus saith the Lord of Hosts, the God of Israel: Behold, I will punish the king of Babylon and his land, as I have punished the king of Assyria, and I will bring Israel again to his habitation; and he shall feed on Carmel and Bashan, and his soul shall be satisfied on Mount Ephraim and Gilead. IN THOSE DAYS, AND IN THAT TIME, saith the Lord, the iniquity of Israel shall be sought for, and there shall be none; and the sins of Judah, and they shall not be found, for I will pardon them whom I reserve."—Jeremiah 1: 1, 3, 4, 5, 18.

The co-incidence of the two events, thus so circumstantially set forth, is here affirmed by the God of Israel Himself, in terms as explicit and direct as language is capable of affording. If the occurrence of two synchronous events be not described in the above Scripture, by what language could it be described? If it will not bear the construction we have placed upon it, what construction would it bear? The words, "IN THOSE DAYS, AND IN THAT TIME," occurring in both passages and l'nking both events together, as co-incident in point of time, are perfectly definite. They are neither figurative nor enigmatic.

Now, if these events have not taken place in the past, they must, as truly as God liveth, take place in the future. This is no less true than that, take place when they will, they will take place together, or so nearly together as justly to be pronounced co-incident in the prophetic Scriptures.

If, therefore, the two families of the House of Israel have not, as yet, been jointly restored to their own land, and forgiven and blest as an undivided nation therein, according to the conditions and circumstances predicted by Jeremiah, and their re-union sealed by a "perpetual covenant" with the Lord, then cannot the city of Babylon have been destroyed and the city and land of Babylon have been desolated, according to the predictions cited. It is this latter point, that more especially engages our attention in the present chapter.

Their predicted restoration is clearly and unquestionably *future*. For when, since the revolt of the ten tribes under Jeroboam, have the "children of Israel, they and the children of Judah together," sought the Lord and entered into a "perpetual covenant" with him? Speculation was never more at a loss than at this very day, as to who or where the ten tribes are. Nor, on the other hand, was it ever less at a loss. No fact, in the history of God's providence, has ever been wrapped in obscurity more profound, more mysterious, more impenetrable, than the identity, and abode or abodes, of the ten outcast tribes of Israel, from the beginning of their captivity even until now. Human curiosity and speculation have never been more completely baffled by the inscrutable purposes of the Divine will. The concealment has been, and still is, as profound and effectual on the one hand, as the manifestation predicted by Jeremiah will be patent and glorious on the other. There will be no mistaking the event when it occurs, as there could be none, if it had occurred already.

Earnest advocates are not wanting of theories that traces of the lost tribes are to be discovered in Armenia, Nestoria, Persia, and other regions of Asia. On the other hand, Lord Kingsborough devoted forty years of a most valuable life, and no inconsiderable portion of a most princely fortune, to researches into Mexican antiquities, which tend to show that the ancient Aztecs and other Indian tribes are their descendants. The Roman Catholic and other European museums opened to him all the treasures of their archives. The co-incidences adduced by him, of many of their religious and social rites and customs with those of the ancient Hebrews, are most striking and impressive. His theory, though confused, is, perhaps, the most plausible of all, but, after all, and like all, it is a theory only. God, who unfolds his own counsels at his own sovereign pleasure only, has never unlocked that secret to mortal ken.

Wherefore if the "outcasts of Israel" have never yet, hand in hand with the "dispersed of Judah," set their faces Zionward, and been reëstablished, forgiven and blest as one nation in their own land, then also cannot the co-incident and final destruction of Babylon, as described by Jeremiah, have yet occurred.

The converse inference — namely, that the "dispersed of Judah" never having been restored, so also the "outcasts of Israel" can not have been — is equally legitimate, and equally conclusive of the futurity of the final destruction of Babylon.

Again; Christ assured the Jews that they should be "trodden under foot of the Gentiles, until the times of the Gentiles should be fulfilled." Now if the predictions of Jeremiah, which we have quoted, concerning the restoration of the Jews, have been fulfilled in the past, then also must the "times of the Gentiles" have been fulfilled in the past. But most clearly, the "times of the Gentiles" are still unfulfilled. The Jews must therefore still be trodden under foot, for they can not, at one and the same time, be scattered and trodden under foot, and restored, re-established, forgiven and blest, as a nation. Such a supposition would be as illogical and absurd, as it would be contrary to the plainest facts of history, and every day's observation.

When the times of the Gentiles are fulfilled; when that promise of God to Israel is redeemed, "Behold, I will take the children of Israel from among the Gentiles, whither they be gone, and will gather them on every side, and bring them into their own land;" and when that other promise of God to Israel is also redeemed, "It shall come to pass in that day, that the Lord shall set his hand again the second time, to recover the remnant of his people which shall be left from Assyria, and from Egypt, and from Pathros, and from Cush, and from Elam, and from Shinar, and from Hamath, and from the isles of the sea, and he shall set up an ensign for the nations, and shall assemble the outcasts of Israel, and gather together the dispersed of Judah [how wholly unfulfilled in the past!] from the four corners of the earth;" then it is that the curse, which has hung so long and so heavily over the devoted heads of this suffering but chosen people, will be lifted; then it is that they will be "settled after their old estates," renationalized, forgiven and blest; then it is, but not till then, that the city and land of Babylon will be finally desolated, and the king of Babylon destroyed; then it is, but not till then, that the whole House of Israel will, as predicted, "rule over her oppressors," and take up her triumphal song, "How hath the oppressor ceased—the golden city ceased!" The return of re-united Israel and her triumphal reign over her oppressors will be as literal, as conspicuous to the observation of the whole earth, as have been her dispersion and her persecutions. We do not see, with such plain declarations of God before us, what principle of reasoning, or what method of interpretation can, with scriptural safety, reach an opposite conclusion. Deny the literal future of Israel, as predicted by Isaiah and Jeremiah, and we are compelled, in all logical fairness, to deny, not less, her literal present and literal past, which would be absurd.

Observe further the following prediction of Isaiah:

"The Lord will have mercy upon Jacob, and will yet choose Israel, and set them in their own land, and the strangers shall be joined with them, and they shall cleave to the house of Jacob. And the peoples [the Gentile nations] shall take them and bring them to their place; and the house of Israel shall possess them in the land of the Lord, for servants and handmaids; and they shall rule over their oppressors. And it shall come to pass, IN THE DAY [not before] that the Lord shall give thee rest from thy sorrow, and thy fear, and from the hard bondage wherein thou wast made to serve, that thou shalt take up this parable against the king of Babylon, and say, How hath the oppressor ceased—the golden city ceased!"—Isaiah xiv. 1—4.

When have Israel been carried back to their place by the Gentile nations? When have they taken them captives whose captives they were? When have they had rest from their sorrow, and their fear, and the hard bondage wherein they have been made to serve, and are serving still? When have they ruled over their oppressors? But a remnant only of the two tribes of Judah and Benjamin were restored by Cyrus at the close of the Babylonian captivity, and instead of ruling over him, they were ruled over by him, while the whole house of Jacob, and a portion of the house of Judah (comprehending always the tribe of Benjamin) remained dispersed among the Gentiles. And yet we are expressly assured that all these events are either to precede or accompany the final destruction of Babylon.

A recent writer has urged that the predictions of restoration and blessing to Israel and the co-incident and final destruction of Babylon have been fulfilled, because they were uttered by Isaiah and Jeremiah antecedently to the restoration from Babylon under Cyrus. But was the nation, both branches of it, fully re-collected and finally forgiven then? Have they suffered nothing for unforgiven sins since? Have not the "outcasts of Israel" remained outcast, and the "dispersed of Judah" dispersed since? Have they not been a "peeled nation," terribly chastised of heaven, ever since? Has not that added, that most terrible curse of all, self-invoked while their hands were red with the blood of the murdered Messiah, "His blood be on us and on our children," been fulfilled with a terribleness with which no curse was ever fulfilled before? Is it not fulfilling still? When, since the return from Babylon of a portion only of two of the twelve tribes, could the iniquity of Israel be sought for, and there was none; and the sins of Judah, and they not be found? When has there been heard such violence in her land, such wasting and destruction within her borders, as since their return from the waters of Babylon? Then have not the predictions of these prophets concerning Israel and Babylon been accomplished. Then hath not " Babylon, the glory of kingdoms, the beauty of the Chaldees' excellency, become as when God overthrew Sodom and Gomorrah." *

So also the prophet Joel, describing the mustering of the armies of the prophetic earth at Armageddon for the final siege of Jerusalem, which will be co-incident in time with the final destruction of Babylon by the hordes of central and northern Asia, as will elsewhere be shown, says:

"For, behold, IN THOSE DAYS, AND IN THAT TIME, when I shall bring again the captivity of Judah and Jerusalem, I will also gather all nations, and will bring them down into the valley of Jehoshaphat, and will plead with them there for my people, and for my heritage Israel, whom they have scattered among the nations, and parted my land."

---

* Some learned and excellent writers, such as Cumming, Seiss, and many others, may object to our view, because our Lord assured His disciples that, at His second advent, He should come " as a thief," that is, with the suddenness and unexpectedness of a thief, "in the night," " as a snare," "in an hour that ye think not," &c., and because, this indefinite postponing of his coming robs it of its unexpectedness. Not at all. The apostate nations of the prophetic earth, and the sleeping virgins of His church, deceived by Antichrist's counterfeit millennium, will expect Him less even then, than now. The intermediate restoration of Babylon and the delusive glories of her system will cause His coming to be, not less, but all the more unexpected, all the more a snare.

This passage fixes, most definitely, the precise period of the final destruction of Babylon.

If, therefore, the captivity of Israel and Jerusalem has not been "brought again," as we know it has not, then, interpreting Isaiah, Jeremiah and Joel together, or, rather, allowing them to interpret one another, it is altogether safe to say that Babylon has not, as yet, been visited with her final doom.

But our argument rests not here. It would be incomplete, if we failed to notice the harmony of history with prophecy. Even if the past destruction of Babylon and the present condition of her ruins appeared to answer to the maledictions of prophecy, still it is none the less certain that their final fulfillment must be future, so long as the two families of the House of Israel remain outcast, their organized nationality unrestored, and their sins unforgiven. But they do not so answer, or so appear to answer.

What are these maledictions, and how far, if at all, have they been fulfilled?

"Her cities are a desolation, a dry land, and a wilderness, a land wherein no man dwelleth, neither doth any son of man pass thereby."—Jeremiah li. 43.

"Because of the wrath of the Lord, it shall not be inhabited, but it shall be wholly desolate."—Jeremiah l: 13.

"For every purpose of the Lord shall be performed against Babylon, to make the land of Babylon a desolation without an inhabitant."—Jeremiah li. 29.

"And they shall not take of thee a stone for a corner, nor a stone for foundations; but thou shalt be desolate FOR EVER, saith the Lord."—Jeremiah li. 26.

"And Babylon, the glory of kingdoms, the beauty of

the Chaldees' excellency, shall be as when God overthrew Sodom and Gomorrah. It shall NEVER be inhabited, neither shall it be dwelt in from generation to generation; neither shall the Arabian pitch tent there."—Isaiah xiii. 19, 20.

Bold as the statement may appear, and contravening, as it does, the cherished belief of so many thousand good and faithful Christians of all these tarrying ages, that these predictions have been already fulfilled, and indeed, that they are to be classed among the very highest completed evidences of the verity of prophecy, and the infallibility of God's Word; yet it is nevertheless true, that not one of these prophecies has ever yet been fulfilled. God's providence in history is a not less infallible teacher than the revelations of His Word. They can not conflict or disagree. Their testimony, if carefully sought for, will always be found concurrent and harmonious. "Her cities" have never, in point of fact, been " a desolation, a dry land, and a wilderness, where no man dwelleth, neither doth any son of man pass thereby." Thousands upon thousands of the sons of men have passed and continually pass thereby, have crossed and re-crossed her ruins, throughout their whole extent, in every possible direction. Thousands upon thousands of Arabians have, not only casually pitched their tents, but taken up their abodes there, which, in turn, have been inhabited by their children and their children's children, " from generation to generation." Within the last seventy years, many European travellers of high note and unquestioned authority, among whom may be named Rich, Buckingham, Ker Porter, Keppel, Loftus, Mignan, Chesney and Layard, have carefully traversed and explored her ruins in all directions, and always *under Arabian escort*. The ruins of Babylon contain, in their very midst, the Arab city of Hillah, having a population of ten thousand inhabitants, the brick and stone composing whose " corners " and "foundations" as also the "corners" and " foundations " of Seleucia, Ctesiphon, Kúfa, Kerbellah, Bághdád, and other cities in the neighborhood, have been taken from the ruins of Babylon. Not a few of the inhabitants of her ruins find their livelihood, as brick and stone masons, by quarrying the ruins for this very purpose. This is proved by the testimony of every traveller who has visited the district of Hillah.* There are also several Arab villages, inhabited partly in tents, within the limits of the ruins. The site of the ancient city, which is said to have been sixty miles in circumference, is dotted with extensive gardens and date groves, which latter are said to be far superior to those of Egypt and the finest in the world; also with fruitful wheat and rice fields ; and, as long ago as 1812, yielded, as Rich informs us, an annual tribute to its Turkish masters of 300,000 piasters. † Colonel Ches-

---

* See, for example, Mignan's Travels in Chaldea, p. 177 : "Some of the ravines [of the ruins of Babylon] are full sixty feet deep, which may principally be attributed to the Arabs, who were constantly at work to obtain the valuable *bricks*, which, from the vicinity of the river, are with little trouble and expense conveyed to Hillah, or any towns north or south."

† Rich, describing Hillah and the site of the ruins of Babylon, says: " The gardens on both sides of the river [Euphrates] are very extensive, so that the town appears embosomed in a wood of date trees. The air is salubrious, and the soil extremely fertile, producing great quantities of rice, dates, and grain of different kinds, though it is not cultivated to above half the degree of which it is susceptible. The grand cause of this fertility is the Euphrates."

Major Skinner, who visited it in 1835, thus describes his approach to Hillah: "I crossed by a bridge of boats to the west side, which was broad and firm, over which I measured one hundred and seventy paces, giving to the breadth of the Euphrates more than four hundred feet. The bridge was naturally a great thoroughfare, and I passed it in company with many on horseback and on foot. The reach of the river below the bridge reflected the rays of the setting sun, which had just

ney, who surveyed the Euphratean country in the years 1835, 1836, and 1837, under a commission from the British Government, says, "an Arabian tribe were encamped in the very midst of the ruins, during the whole time of my sojourn there."

Again; not the least striking feature of the predicted destruction of Babylon is its *suddenness*.

"Babylon hath been a golden cup in the Lord's hand, that made all the earth drunken; the nations have drunken of her wine; therefore the nations are mad."

"Babylon is SUDDENLY fallen and destroyed: howl for her."—Jeremiah li. 7, 8.

"Therefore shall her plagues come IN ONE DAY, death, and mourning, and famine; and she shall be utterly burned with fire."

"Alas, alas that great city, that was clothed in fine linen, and purple, and scarlet, and decked with gold, and precious stones, and pearls! for IN ONE HOUR so great riches is come to naught."

"Alas, alas that great city, wherein were made rich all that had ships in the sea by reason of her costliness! for IN ONE HOUR is she made desolate."

"And a mighty angel took up a stone like a great millstone, and cast it into the sea, saying, Thus with violence shall that great city Babylon be thrown down, and shall be found no more at all."—Rev. xviii. 8, 16, 17, 19, 21.

turned everything to gold, and the long rows of date trees really glittered in the bosom of the stream."

Buckingham thus describes his approach to Hillah: "On gaining the summit of this huge mass [amidst the ruins] we had the first sight of the Euphrates, flowing majestically along through verdant banks, and its serpentine course apparently losing itself in the palm groves of Hillah, whose mosques and minarets we could just perceive about five miles to the southward of us."

Verily, descriptions of anything rather than "a land made desolate, so that no man shall dwell therein!"

"And it shall be, when thou hast made an end of reading this book, that thou shalt bind a stone to it, and cast it into the midst of the Euphrates: and thou shalt say, Thus [thus suddenly and violently] shall Babylon sink, and not rise from the evil that I will bring upon her."— Jer. li. 63, 64.

But the predictions of the *suddenness* have not been any more fulfilled than those of the *fulness* of her destruction. There is nothing in history that tends, in the slightest degree, to verify either of these required conditions of her final destruction. That Babylon has been destroyed, no one will deny, but that her destruction was the result, not of sudden violence, but of gradual declension, is equally undeniable.

"At the noise of the taking of Babylon, the earth is moved, and the cry is heard among the nations—Babylon is suddenly fallen and destroyed." Jeremiah 1: 46. But the earth was never moved less by any event than by the taking of Babylon by Cyrus. All that is said of it in Scripture is, "In that night was Belshazzar, the king of the Chaldeans, slain, and Darius, the Mede, took the kingdom." Daniel v. 31. It was no destruction of the city. It was anything rather than suddenly destroyed. It was the simple occupation of the throne of Babylon by one person instead of another, a quiet transfer of power from one dynasty to another, without commotion or violence, or any considerable destruction or slaughter. The sentries of the king were the only victims. Herodotus relates that (Cyrus having taken the city in the night) it was not till three hours after sunrise that the inhabitants of quarters distant from the palace knew they were living under a Persian satrapy. *More than two hundred years* after the capture of the city by Cyrus, so far from having been suddenly destroyed at that or any subsequent period, it was, under the reign of Alexander, one of the chief cities of the East, the metropolis of his dominion. St. Peter wrote his epistle there in the sixty-fifth year of the Christian era, more than six hundred years after the capture of the city by Cyrus. Long after the establishment of Christianity, the patriarch of Babylon was one of the great ecclesiastical rulers of the East. Four hundred and sixty years after Christ, Theodoret speaks of Babylon as being inhabited in part, by Jews. Five hundred years after Christ, the famous Babylonian Talmud was promulgated. Nine hundred and seventeen years after Christ, Babel is mentioned as a small village on the site of Babylon. The city of Hillah, before referred to, was enlarged and fortified eleven hundred years after Christ. Skinner speaks of Hillah as a city, in eighteen hundred and thirty-three, of twelve thousand inhabitants. Not long since a bishop of Babylon was consecrated by the Pope.

No period in the declension of Babylon has ever been marked by any of the attending signs and tokens, so numerously connected in Scripture with its sudden, its utter, its final, overthrow.

But what profiteth it to multiply evidence, to show that the predictions of Isaiah and Jeremiah, concerning the final destruction of Babylon, have never been fulfilled?

Babylon has never been that great maritime and commercial city described in the eighteenth chapter of the Revelation. She was anything rather than a city of merchants in the days of Chaldea, Persia, Greece, or Rome.

Wherefore, we affirm that Babylon, before she can be

destroyed according to the predictions of Isaiah, Jeremiah and the apostle John, than the fulfilment of which nothing can be more certain, *must first be restored*. That she will be restored in more than her ancient splendor, and be the crowning glory of our Gentile civilization, we can in no wise doubt, when we remember the words with which the apostle of the Revelation records her final doom. It must not be forgotten that he reveals only the *closing scenes* of the present dispensation, thus establishing, beyond a question, the *futurity* of the final destruction of Babylon.

"After these things I saw another angel, coming down from heaven, having great authority; and the earth was lightened with his glory. And he cried with a mighty voice, saying, Fallen, fallen is Babylon the great, ... because by reason of the wrath of her fornication all the nations have fallen, and the kings of the earth committed fornication with her, and the merchants of the earth waxed rich through the power of her delicacies. . . . . Because she saith in her heart, 'I sit a queen and am not a widow, and shall see no mourning.' Therefore IN ONE DAY shall her plagues come, death, and mourning, and famine, and she shall be utterly burned with fire, because mighty is the Lord who judged her. . . . . And the merchants of the earth weep and mourn, ... and every shipmaster, and every passenger, and sailors, and as many as trade by the sea, stood afar off, and cried when they saw the smoke of her burning, saying, 'what city is like unto the great city, ... alas! alas the great city, wherein were made rich all that had ships in the sea, by reason of her costliness! because IN ONE HOUR was she made desolate.' And a mighty angel took up a stone, like a great mill-stone, and cast it into the sea, saying, 'Thus with violence shall the great city Babylon be thrown down, and shall no more be found at all.'"

The Babylon here described, for so Scripture expressly and repeatedly assures us, is Babylon "in the land of Chaldea," not, as some have supposed, Rome in the land of Italy. We have been able to discover in Scripture no color of evidence that there are two cities described therein with the name of Babylon common to both. It appears to us a wholly fanciful and unwarranted substitution of names. The prophets Isaiah and Jeremiah, as if effectually to forestall any such substitution, are most careful uniformly to locate the Babylon whose destruction they foretell, in Chaldea. As for instance: "Come down and sit in the dust, O virgin daughter of Babylon, sit on the ground: there is no throne, *O daughter of the Chaldeans*, for thou shalt no more be called tender and delicate, ... sit thou silent, and get thee into darkness, *O daughter of the Chaldeans:* for thou shalt no more be called the lady of kingdoms."

CHAPTER III.

THE SYMBOLIC BABYLON OF PROPHECY.

ITS COMPOSITE CHARACTER, INCLUDING, NOT ROMANISM ONLY, BUT ALL FORMS OF FALSE RELIGION AND INFIDELITY.

THE eighteenth chapter of the Revelation describes the literal Babylon, the seventeenth the symbolic Babylon, of prophecy.

Two of the most notable symbols of prophetic Scripture are presented in the seventeenth chapter, those of the "*woman*" and the "*beast.*" The beast is the same as described in the seventh chapter of Daniel, and has been sufficiently referred to in a preceding chapter. But the woman, in the present prophetic connection, is a symbol peculiar to the prophet of the Revelation, and is thus described.

"And there came one of the seven angels who had the seven bowls, and talked with me, saying, Come hither; I will shew unto thee the judgment of the great harlot that sitteth upon many waters, with whom the kings of the earth committed fornication, and the inhabitants of the earth were made drunk with the wine of her fornication. And he carried me away into the wilderness in the spirit: and I saw a woman sitting upon a scarlet beast, full of names of blasphemy, having seven heads and ten horns. And the woman was clothed in purple and scarlet, and decked with gold, and precious stones and pearls, having a cup of gold in her hand full of abominations—and the filthiness of her fornication, and upon her forehead a name written, a MYSTERY, BABYLON THE GREAT, THE MOTHER OF THE HARLOTS AND THE ABOMINATIONS [IDOLATRIES] OF THE EARTH."—Rev. xvii. 1—5. Tregelles' Translation.

Woman is the invariable Scripture symbol of a moral system, good or evil. The woman here described is the symbol of a manifestly and to the last and most opprobrious degree evil system. She is seen sitting upon a scarlet colored beast, and is at first represented as his mistress, guiding and controlling him. He is her servant, obsequious to her will, and upholds and supports her; but, afterwards, when she has served his purposes sufficiently, when he no longer requires her aid and her enchantments, when he is able to assert and maintain supreme dominion without them, then " the ten horns which thou sawest [which are symbols of the ten kings of the prophetic earth] and the beast [καὶ τὸ θηρίον], these shall *hate the harlot, and shall make her desolate and naked, and shall eat her flesh, and burn her with fire. For God hath put into their hearts to fulfil his mind [and to make one mind], and to give their kingdom unto the beast, until the words of God shall be completed.*"—Rev. xvii. 16, 17. Tregelles' Translation.

Wherefore it appears that the woman is to be destroyed when this last and sole despot of the prophetic earth shall, through her agency, and by means of her allurements, have brought the ten kingdoms, into which the Roman earth will then have been divided, into subjection to that dominion of which he will be the imperial head, "glorifying himself as God," "until the words of God shall be fulfilled."

Who is this woman, and who the beast? The former inquiry we propose to answer in this chapter, the latter in the chapter next following.

But, first, we will endeavor to define, with more strict and careful precision, the specific sphere of their dominion.

Her dominion, so far as it is described in the above chapter, is only referred to as co-extensive with his, not as exceeding it.

His dominion will be the prophetic earth of Daniel and the Revelation, as defined in a former chapter. It will, be well, for the sake of greater definiteness, to enumerate, under their modern names, the countries and provinces included within the Roman earth, the identity of which with the prophetic earth has been shown.

The Roman empire (which first assumed its full imperial standing in succession to Greece when Augustus Cæsar conquered Cleopatra) attained its widest territorial development under Trajan. The following is a list of the countries then included within its limits.*

IN WESTERN AND NORTH-WESTERN EUROPE.

England and Scotland: *not* Ireland.
Spain and Portugal.
France and Savoy.
Belgium and parts of Holland west of the Rhine.
Luxembourg and Bavarian territory west of the Rhine.
Rhenish Prussia west of the Rhine.

* We adopt the enumeration of Dr. B. W. Newton.

Baden, Wurtemberg, and the southern half of Bavaria. Switzerland.

IN SOUTHERN AND SOUTH-EASTERN EUROPE.

Italy.

Greece.

All the islands of the Mediterranean.

Turkey in Europe south of the Danube, including Bosnia, Servia and Bulgaria.

Austrian provinces south of the Danube, including the southwestern wing of Hungary and that part of the Banat which lies east of the Roman Vallum.

Transylvania, Wallachia, Moldavia, and Bessarabia; these four countries being situate north of the Danube, and answering to Trajan's province of Dacia.

IN ASIA.

The Turkish dominions, taking Assyria as the most easterly province, and an imaginary line skirting the north of Arabia to Egypt as the southern limit. This division includes, of course, Palestine and Asia Minor.

IN AFRICA.

· Egypt and the whole northern coast, namely, Barca, Tripoli, Tunis, Algeria, Morocco and Fez; Sallé, a little outside of the straits of Gibraltar, being the most westerly city.

Such are the countries that fall within the "*Orbis Terrarum*" of the Romans: the Πᾶσα ἡ οἰκουμένη of Scripture; such the prophetic earth of Daniel and the Revelation; such the sphere of the dominion of the woman and the beast; such the boundaries of their empire. We would not imply that their *influence* will be circumscribed with that rigid and absolute precision which these limits would indicate, or that it will not be widely and destructively felt beyond them; but we speak now only of the predicted sphere within which, according to prophetic Scripture, they will bear rule.

The reign of the woman and the beast, in their accomplished supremacy of dominion, is clearly future.

It has been supposed by some that the beast is a symbol of Pagan Rome, and the woman of Paganism. This can not be, for the prophet of the Revelation expressly assures us that the beast "*is to ascend*" (μέλλει ἀναβαίνειν), whereas, when the prophet wrote, Pagan Rome had already ascended to the height of its power.

It has also been supposed that the beast represents Papal Rome, and the woman the Papacy. But this supposition must be equally erroneous, for the same prophet no less expressly declares that "the ten horns *and the beast* (καὶ τὸ θηρίο) these shall hate the harlot, and shall make her desolate and naked, and shall eat her flesh and burn her with fire." Rev. xvii. 16. If, therefore, the latter supposition were true, it would involve the necessity of the Pope's destroying the Papacy, in order to exalt himself to supreme dominion, as Pope, which would be absurd.

Again; the reign of the woman and the beast must be future, for what sovereign system, symbolised by the woman, reigns, or has ever reigned, over ten kings of the prophetic earth? When has the prophetic earth, the territory of the Roman Empire (eastern and western divisions together), been divided into ten separate and independent kingdoms, or been ruled over by ten confederated and conspiring kings, and they been subject to a single sovereign, to whom they have concurred to "give their kingdoms until the words of God shall be fulfilled," and with whom they have concurred to hate and destroy that system? What single sovereign wears, or has ever worn, these ten prophetic diadems, or held these ten prophetic realms subject to his sceptre? If such a system and such a sovereign have existed not in the past, and exist not now, then must their predicted reign be future, what types so ever have signified, or may now signify, their character or their appearing.

The Papacy furnishes no evidence of any drift in this direction. The confluent floods of a system so comprehensive, so all-embracing, as symbolic Babylon, can never flow in so shallow a channel, between banks so narrow, or be impeded by the opposing but ineffectual waves of so confined and exclusive an ecclesiasticism. Modern tendencies set overwhelmingly in other directions. The Papacy can not hold her own at their side, excepting as a concurring force? And, surely, the channel is deep enough and the stream wide enough for all, for symbolic Babylon is the mother not of this harlot, or of that, only,—not the slightest limitation in this regard is intimated by the prophet—but of ALL the harlots, of ALL the evil systems. So prolific and comprehensive a maternity can not be predicated of any one known system, of Romanism, or of Judaism, or of Mohammedanism, or of the Greek Church, or of Hindooism, or of any or all forms of infidel protestantism, or of any or all forms of ritualism or ecclesiasticism, most of all of one so exclusive, so unsympathetic, so jealous and exacting, so offensive to its sister harlots, as Romanism. What more improbable, not to say impossible, in the light of present tendencies, than that any one of the systems thus named or referred to should ever absorb and become the sovereign mistress of all? No! the exclusiveness of each and every one of these systems excludes it from so extended sway, from that universality of dominion ascribed to symbolic Babylon. "*And in her was found the blood of prophets, and of saints, and of* ALL *that have been slain upon the earth.*"—Rev. xviii. 24.

Nor, if it were probable, which, from present appearances, is not in the least so, that Romanism, or any one of these systems, would ever become co-extensive with the prophetic or Roman earth, would it be possible that the stain of exclusive and universal blood-guiltiness should ever rest upon Romanism, or upon any one of these systems, which system so ever may have shed, or shall shed, the most blood. The blood which Paganism has shed can never be said to attach to Romanism. No more can the blood which Judaism, or Hindooism, or Mohammedanism, or the Greek Church, or an infidel protestantism, or any other evil system, has shed, or may shed, be said to attach to her. To no city which Romanism has ever occupied, or can occupy, as her ecclesiastical seat and metropolitan centre, can so solitary a preëminence, so unshared a monopoly, of blood-guiltiness, be said to attach; certainly so long as she remains true to her record, and so long as her present characteristics and disposition remain unchanged, nor ever, indeed, unless, forsooth, she should so loosen the iron fetters of her ecclesiasticism, and so extend the shelter of her wings, as, not to tolerate only, but to absorb and concentrate within herself, so as to make wholly her own, and contract and assume the proper responsibility, and respective guilt, of each and all the other evil systems and forms of harlotry, from the lowest and most debased of Paganism, to the highest and most refined of an infidel and self-glorifying protestantism. She must become the fond, the loving, the accredited foster-mother alike of the Jewish and the Greek, the Hindoo and the Mohammedan, and all other abominations. They, and, with them, the ten kings and the inhabitants of the prophetic earth, must joyfully accept, and be made drunk by, the golden cup of the wine of the wrath of her fornication. She must brood with as fond and solicitous a maternity over the polished Pagan worshippers of Mars' Hill, as over kings and priests and long trains of lowlier worshippers within the courts of her own temples. She must bow as supple a knee to the Jupiter Ultor of the Pantheon, as to the paintings and frescoes of the Vatican. She must know no difference in her lustful embrace, between the juggling priests of the East, the licentious fetich worshippers of the South, and the learned and polite, but conceited and scornful, defamers and defiers of the divinity of Jesus, " speaking great and blasphemous things against the Most High " from the chairs of the protestant academies of the West. She must accept, nothing loth, the transfer to her own skirts of all the stains of blood-guiltiness to be found upon the skirts of all her sister harlots, for in her, if she be symbolic Babylon, must be found the " blood of prophets, and of saints, and of *all* that have been slain upon the earth." Ah no! Romanism has in reserve for her no future such as this. No tokens, not the remotest, of such a destiny are to be discerned. The " Mores Catholici," the " Ages of Faith," are past.

Who, then, *is* this woman of the Revelation, this

mother of [*all*] the harlots, and [*all*] the abominations of the earth"?

We have located the sphere of her dominion, and defined its boundaries. We have rendered certain the futurity of her reign. We have seen who she is not and can not be. But does not Scripture reveal to us who she is, any sign by which we may identify her presence or discern her approach? Most assuredly. The woman hath her types and her precursors not fewer nor less notable than the beast. More than this, her exact lineaments can be quite as precisely and unmistakably traced and defined.

In the first place, she is to be inseparably associated, if not absolutely identified, with a world-wide commercial system, of proportions more grand, more deftly harmonized, more glorious (according to the standards of earthly glory), than the world has ever seen.

The prophet Zechariah had a vision of her, considered in this aspect. "Then the angel that talked with me went forth, and said unto me, Lift up now thine eyes and see what is this that goeth forth. And I said, What is it? And he said, This is an ephah that goeth forth. He said moreover, This is their resemblance [aspect or appearance.] through all the earth. And, behold, then there was lifted up a talent [weighty piece] of lead; and this is the woman that sitteth in the midst of the ephah. And he said, This is wickedness. And he cast it into the midst of the ephah; and he cast the weight of lead upon the mouth thereof. Then I lifted up mine eyes and looked, and, behold, there came out two women, and the wind was in their wings; for they had wings like the wings of a stork: and they lifted up the ephah between the earth and the heaven. Then said I to the angel that talked with me, Whither do they bear the ephah? And he said unto me, To build it an house in the land of Shinar; and it shall be established and set there upon her own base."

The ephah was a Hebrew measure of all kinds of solids and liquids, equivalent to about seven and a half gallons of our measure. It was the Hebrew emblem of commerce, the symbol of merchants. The ephah of this vision, when first seen by the prophet, was in motion, "going forth." Afterwards, though at first invisible (being concealed therein by a weighty cover of lead) the cover being removed, a woman (the remembered symbol of a moral system) is disclosed to the view of the prophet, sitting in the midst of the ephah. After which the angel casts into the ephah another woman, who is named by the angel "wickedness." He then casts upon the ephah its cover of lead, concealing both from the prophet's sight. Finally (and we are now introduced to the sequel of the vision, to the *closing events* symbolized by it) the two women are seen to break forth from their confinement, to exalt their haughty symbol between the earth and the heaven, and to bear it, with swift wings and strong. Where? "To the land of Shinar." Wherefore? "To build it an house there, to establish it, and set her upon her own base there."

We have, therefore, in this vision, first, the symbol, not of a commercial system only, but of a *vast* commercial system, for "this is their resemblance through all the earth." We are next introduced to the moral systems which, under the symbol of the two women, are seen to inhabit that system; which assume the sovereign control of it; which actuate and inspire it; which direct and determine its movements; which build for it an house, a literal city, and establish for it a dwelling place. That city is declared to be on the plains of Shinar, on the banks of the Euphrates, in the land of Babylon.

Now Zechariah is preëminently a latter day prophet. He details, to a more remarkable and circumstantial extent than, perhaps, any other Old Testament prophet, those scenes which are to be immediately associated with the conversion and the dawning of the millennial glory of the House of Israel. The vision of the ephah must, therefore, have specific connection with those scenes, with that period of the world's history in which they will occur. It teaches us that not the sceptre, or the sword, or the mitre, but the *ephah* is the appointed symbol of that period; that at least one of its chief characteristics will be a colossal, world-wide and most imposing commercial system; that that system will have been controlled, and will doubtless be controlled unto the very end, by two women, two moral systems, and that the name of one of them will be " WICKEDNESS."

Turn now to the apostle Paul. In discoursing to the Thessalonians of the second coming of our Saviour, he says (we translate literally from the Greek):

"That day [the day of the Lord] will not commence except there first come the apostasy; and the man of sin be revealed, the son of perdition [the 'beast'?] . . . . . Ye know that at at present there is that which restraineth [the talent of lead that covered the ephah?] in order that he might be revealed in his appointed season. For the mystery [and 'upon her forehead a name was written, Mystery.'] of *wickedness* (ἀνομίας, lawlessness) [of her who was cast by the angel into the ephah?] is already working [so prevalent when the apostle wrote, among the Sadducees, the Herodians, the Athenians and others], only there is at present one that restraineth [the angel who cast the talent of lead upon the mouth of the ephah?], until it become developed out of the midst [out of the midst of what? the ephah?] and then shall the wicked one [ὁ ἄνομος, the lawless one, the masculine of ἀνομία, "wickedness"] be revealed, whom the Lord shall consume by the breath of his mouth, and destroy by the brightness of his coming."—2 Thess. ii. 3—9.

What is this but an immaterially differing account of one and the same order of events predicted by Zechariah? What but a reciprocal interpretation, the one prophet by the other?

Turn again to the great New Testament prophet of the closing scenes of the present dispensation. He describes the harlot. He calls her by name. He locates her on the plains of Shinar, on the banks of the Euphrates, in the land of Babylon, seated in her own house, established on her own base. He makes her house the great merchant city of the earth, "whose merchants are princes," the metropolis of a world's commerce, reigned over by her as its sovereign mistress, entertaining, in her satanic hospitality, and making drunk with the wine of the wrath of her fornication, the kings and inhabitants of the apostate Roman earth.

"All that have ships in the sea will be made rich by reason of her costliness . . . . and every ship-master, and every passenger, and sailors, and as many as trade by the sea [will be there] . . . . and merchandise, the merchandise of gold, and of silver, and precious stones, and of pearls, and of fine linen, and of purple and of scarlet and all thyine wood, and every vessel of ivory, and every vessel of most precious wood, and of brass, and of iron and of marble, and of cinnamon, and spice, and odors, and ointment, and frankincense and wine, and oil, and fine flour and wheat, and cattle and sheep, and of horses, and of chariots, and of the bodies and souls of men."—Rev. xviii.

Such will be the house of the ephah in the land of Shinar.

Dr. Chalmers, commenting upon this passage from the Revelation, says: " Revelation xviii. What can be the city here spoken of? It is much liker London than Rome —a commercial than a mere ecclesiastical capital. The lamentation of the kings for Babylon point more to the ecclesiastical capital of their monarchies, whereas the description of her wealth and merchandise point greatly more to our own London. The lamentation of the sailors points more to a place of great shipping interest than to Rome or any place in Italy, and strengthens the argument for its being the capital of our own land. We can not observe that shipmasters are much engaged by the traffic of Rome; and their lamentation seems far more applicable to London, lapsed, it may be, when the period of this fulfilment comes round, into Antichristianism. The merchants of our own land are far more the great men of the earth than those of any other nation."—Sabbath Scripture Readings, vol. iv., p. 423.

Now it will not be denied, in view of this and abundant other evidence to the same effect, in view, indeed, of the knowledge and observation of all, that England is, at present, the chief representative centre of the commerce of the world; or that London is an understood synonym for, so to speak, the capital of a vast, world-wide, and more and more increasingly venal, commercial system. Not, by any means, would we imply, however, that London is, or is destined to be, the literal Babylon of the Revelation, in however impressive a sense she may typify her. In view of the express declarations of prophecy (to which we have already adverted) which locate, with such abundance, precision and certainty of evidence, the literal Babylon of prophecy " in the land of Chaldea," we cannot look upon the supposition of Dr. Chalmers that London may be the prophetic Babylon, as any less fanciful and gratuitous, any less unwarranted by Scripture, than the supposition of others (to which he refers) that Rome is that Babylon. The commercial system of England may be the typical ephah. The presiding genius by which that system is, to so large an extent, animated and controlled, may be the woman first seen sitting in the ephah, not evil in herself at first (commerce is not evil in itself) so far as is revealed or can be inferred, but only as afterwards corrupted by her companion, "wickedness." The ephah may "go forth" from England, may be borne by the swift wings of her commerce to the "land of Shinar;" but its "house" will not be builded in England, any more than in Italy. Its final "base," its last great centre, is no more likely to be established on the banks of the Thames than upon that fanciful cluster of seven hills upon the banks of the yellow Tiber, which men call Rome.*

---

* Says one of the most learned and profound, but not less accurate and cautious classical scholars of England; "The seven *hill*s which originally gave the well-known designation to Rome, were Palatium, Velia, Cermalus, Cœlius, Fagutal, Oppius, Cispius. [So Niebuhr.] The three first of these belonged to the *Palatine*, the two next to the *Cœlian*, and the other two to the *Esquiline*; being thus, in fact, so many ascents, and

We can not doubt that the present commercial system of England presents a more remarkable type of what will be the commercial system of Babylon at the period designated in the eighteenth of the Revelation, than is, or has ever been, presented by any other nation. Many things look strongly in this direction. England and the commercial system of England are interchangeable terms. The English government is the mere creature of her commercial system, and but reflects its spirit and enacts its will. It is the power behind her throne. She, the pretending, or, if you please, the actual, mother of Protestantism, has not only established upon munificent foundations Roman Catholic universities (as witness her Maynooth grant) and educated Roman Catholic priests, but, for the sake of her commerce, has legalized the support of eastern idolatries, and ministered in their temples; paid tribute to the obscene rites of Juggernaut; acknowledged Mohammedanism; presided over the priesthood of Buddha; and forced open the ports of the most populous nation of the earth to her baleful opium trade, surrounding, to this end, with all-powerful safeguards, the most gigantic commercial mo-

not distinct hills. The name of Septicollis [seven-hilled] having been applied to Rome in its early form, was retained long after it ceased to be applicable in its original connection. After Rome had extended, it was supposed by some to relate to seven distinct hills; and thus the *number* was made to correspond by counting the Palatine, Capitoline, Quirinal, Esquiline, Cælian, Aventine, and the trans-Tiberine Janiculum. n this arrangement the Viminal (which lies between the Quirinal and the Esquiline) was omitted, in order not to exceed the number; in another arrangement, Janiculum, as being on the right side of the Tiber, was excluded, and the Viminal reckoned: the seven hills were thus arbitrarily restricted to the left bank of the river, although the hill on the other side is the highest of the whole. In the days of Augustus and his successors, a large part of Rome had extended far beyond the hills and the intervening hollows, into the flat plain of the Campus Martius, which is the site of the greater part of the modern city of the popes." Tregelles' Daniel, pp. 51, 52. The "seven mountains upon which the woman sitteth" (Rev. xvii. 9.) and the "seven heads" of the scarlet beast (Rev. xvii. 3.) can not, therefore, be said, as so many have loosely fancied, to be the seven hills of Rome.

nopoly the world has ever seen. Indeed, as if actually to verify the vision of the ephah, and to " build an house" for it, she has sent out, under a three years' commission, Colonel Chesney, accompanied by a most competent and intelligent staff, gentlemen of high commercial and scientific attainments, to explore, survey, and report upon, the commercial capabilities of the Euphratean country, the land of Shinar itself, and they have reported most favorably.* In running over the record of England in this regard, and counting up a few only of the antichristian enormities of her infidel latitudinarianism, how can we fail to behold in her, at least the beginning of the fulfilment of the vision of the ephah; not a type, merely, but, as it were, the veritable features of the symbolic Babylon of prophecy, "the mother of [all] the harlots, and [all] the abominations of the earth"?

Wherefore, in conclusion, we believe that the symbolic Babylon of prophecy, the harlot of the Revelation, will, in a distinctive and systematic sense, be the moral *animus*, the animating and presiding genius, of a vast, confederated system of governmental policy and power, coextensive with the limits, and having, as the basis of its support, the commercial wealth and energy, of the prophetic earth of Daniel and the Revelation; that it will be the sovereign and acknowedged mistress of that system, and, as such, be glorified, and be a shining, but deceitful and fatal counterfeit of Christ's millennium; that her "costliness" and delicacy of life, administered unto by all that the concentrated governmental power and concentrated commercial wealth of the apostate prophetic earth can confer, and her earthly glory, in all its myriad forms

* See Appendix: Extracts from Col. Chesney's Report.

and appliances, the loftiness of her self-conceit and the meretricious grandeur of her style, will be beyond all former compare; that she will be the last, the proudest, the most magnificent triumph of Gentile civilization, preluding in her pleasant palaces, to the measure of her flutes and soft recorders, the quickly-speeding dominion of the beast, her own fiery judgment, and the final destruction of her queenly capital; that her local and metropolitan centre will be " in the land of Shinar," on the banks of the Euphrates, in the city and land of Babylon; that Antichrist — the " monster" of Daniel, and the " beast" of the Revelation — first wooing and supporting her as his mistress, and ascending into sole and supreme dominion by the aid, in part, of her fascinations, her enchantments and her sorceries, will, in the end, invoking the willing concurrence of the ten confederate kings of the prophetic earth, turn upon and destroy her, and himself thenceforward attract the wonder, and command the homage, and exact the worship of the rulers and the inhabitants of the prophetic earth ("and all that dwell upon the earth shall worship him." — Rev. xiii. 8.), " glorifying himself as God until the words of God shall be fulfilled;" until the Lamb of God, the Prince of Peace, the Messiah of Israel, shall come again, the second time, not as a despised carpenter's son, born in a manger, but as the " stone cut out of the mountain without hands," the King of kings and Lord of lords, whom the heaven of heavens can not contain, to judge and to execute vengeance upon the apostate earth; to render his anger with fury and his rebuke with flames of fire; to gather his living saints, and the departed saints of all the lingering ages, in their risen glory unto himself, to their eternal rest in the heavenly Jerusalem; to re-establish, under a more glorious theocracy than of old, restored and now forgiven Israel in their earthly Jerusalem; and to send forth this ransomed and chosen people upon the sublimest, as it will be the most successful, of earthly missions (of which all present Christian missions are, or can be, but the faintest types,) namely, the redemption, through his blood, not as now, of a "*little flock*"—here a Jew and a Gentile there — but of all the spared inhabitants of the earth.

> "Come, Lord, and tarry not;
> Bring the long-looked-for day:
> Oh! why these years of waiting here,
> These ages of delay!
>
> "Come in thy glorious might,
> Come with the iron rod,
> Scattering thy foes before thy face,
> Thou mighty Son of God.
>
> "Come, and begin thy reign
> Of everlasting peace:
> Come, take the kingdom to thyself,
> Great King of righteousness."

Before dismissing the Babylon, both literal and symbolic, of prophecy, we invite the attention of our readers to a comparison of texts, taken from Isaiah and Jeremiah, on the one hand, and from the Revelation on the other, showing, if it were possible, still more definitely and conclusively, that the Babylon, both literal and symbolic, severally described by them, is identical.

Jer. li. 13. "O thou that dwellest upon many waters, thine end is come, and the measure of thy covetousness."	Rev. xvii. 1. "Come hither, I will show thee the judgment of the great whore, that sitteth upon many waters."
Jer. li. 7. "Babylon hath been a golden cup in the Lord's hand, that made all the earth drunken."	Rev. xvii. 4. "Having a golden cup in her hand full of abominations."
Jer. i. 7. "The nations have drunken of her wine; therefore the nations are mad."	Rev. xvii. 2. "The inhabitants of the earth have been made drunk by the wine of the wrath of her fornication."

It is impossible to properly understand the Babylon, either literal or symbolic, of prophecy, without always noting the difference between them. They are almost alway confounded. The passages just cited refer obviously to symbolic Babylon, and ascribe to her a universality of influence which certainly exceeds any that she has ever exercised or possessed in the past, or possesses now.

Isaiah xlvii. 5. "O daughter of the Chaldeans .... the lady of kingdoms."
Isaiah xiii. 9. "Babylon the glory of kingdoms."
Isaiah xlvii. 7. "Thou saidst, I shall be a lady for ever ... Therefore hear now this, thou that art given to pleasures, that dwellest carelessly, that sayest in thine heart, I am, and none else beside me; I shall not sit as a widow, neither shall I know the loss of children; but these two things shall come to thee *in a moment, in one day*, the loss of children, and widowhood."
Jer. xli. 25. "I will make thee a burnt mountain."
Jer. xli. 45. "My people, go ye out of the midst of her, and deliver ye every man his soul from the fierce anger of the Lord."
Jer. l. 8. "Remove out of the midst of Babylon."
Jer. l. 6. "Flee out of the midst of Babylon."
Jer. li. 9. "For her judgment reacheth unto heaven."
Jer. l. 15. "Take vengeance upon her; as she hath done, do unto her."
Jer. l. 29. "Recompense her according to her work; according to all she hath done, do unto her."
Isaiah xxi. 9. Jer. li. 8. "Babylon is fallen, is fallen. Babylon is sudd'enly fallen and destroyed."
Isaiah xiii. 21. "Wild beasts of the desert shall be there, and their houses shall be full of doleful creatures; and owls shall dwell there, and satyrs (δαιμονια lxx.) shall dance there."

Rev. xviii. 7, 8. "How much she hath glorified herself, and lived deliciously, so much torment and sorrow give her; for she hath said in her heart, I sit a queen, and am no widow, and shall see no sorrow. Therefore shall her plagues come *in one day*, death and mourning, and famine."

Rev. xviii. 8. "She shall be utterly burned with fire."
Rev. xviii. 4. "Come out of her, my people, that ye be not partakers of her sins."

Rev. xviii. 5. "For her sins have reached unto heaven."
Rev. xviii. 6. "Reward her even as she has rewarded you, and double unto her double, according to her works ... in the cup which she hath filled, fill to her double."

Rev. xviii. 2. "Babylon the great is fallen, is fallen."

Rev. xviii. 2. "And is become the habitation of devils, and the hold of every foul spirit, and a cage of every unclean and hateful bird."

Jer. li. 63, 64. "And it shall be, when thou hast made an end of reading this book, that thou shalt bind a stone to it, and cast it into the midst of the Euphrates; and thou shalt say, Thus shalt Babylon sink, and shall not rise from the evil that I will bring upon her."

Rev. xviii. 21. "And a mighty angel took up a stone like to a great millstone, and cast it into the sea, saying, Thus with violence shall that great city Babylon be thrown down, and shall be found no more at all."

The passages last cited and compared, those especially of the eighteenth of the Revelation, refer to the literal Babylon of prophecy. But John describes only the closing scenes of the present dispensation, when Christ will re-appear, at Armageddon, with the armies of heaven following, which event is future. If the evidence thus taken from these three prophets is sufficient to identify the city severally described by them, both literal and symbolic, as being, under each comparison, one and the same city — and who can doubt it without rejecting all rules of evidence? — then must literal Babylon first be restored, and symbolic Babylon still await the full consummation of her predicted reign.

CHAPTER IV.

THE ANTICHRIST OF PROPHECY.

THE RESTORATION OF THE JEWS IN UNBELIEF, AND THEIR SUBSEQUENT PERSECUTION BY ANTICHRIST.

ANTICHRIST is not antichristianism, an abstraction, an unembodied principle, an impersonal idea.

Antichrist is the "beast" of the Revelation; the "little horn" of, respectively, the seventh and eleventh chapters of Daniel; the "king of fierce countenance" of the eighth and "prince that shall come" of the ninth of Daniel; the "king of Assyria" of the tenth, and "king of Babylon" and "Lucifer" of the fourteenth of Isaiah; the "man of sin" and "son of perdition" of the second chapter of the second epistle to the Thessalonians. But he is more conspicuously known and portrayed than, perhaps, under any other title, as the "*beast*" of the Revelation. These, with their accompanying descriptions and portraitures, are separate titles and accounts of one and the same person. That person is the last great monarch of the Gentiles, the Antichrist of prophecy. He is not many persons, or a succession of persons (as, for instance, the Popes of Rome), but one person, having an individuality which is all his own, which no other nor any number of other persons has ever in the least shared, or ever can share, however remarkably they may, in some or in many respects, have answered to the prophetic account of him, have typified his character, or foreshadowed his coming and his career. Antichrist, THE Antichrist, is no more to be regarded in any merely Protean, or generic and representative, or speculative and mystical and spiritualized, sense, than is He, against whom he will finally gather the chosen strength of the armies of the ten confederated kings of the prophetic earth before the walls of Jerusalem, Himself so to be regarded. The antithesis, Christ and Antichrist, is a perfect one, as perfect in its opposing personalities, as in its opposing moral qualities. Thus, for example:

CHRIST.	ANTICHRIST.
John iii. 31. " Comes from above."	Rev. xi. 7. "Comes from below."
John v. 43. " Comes in his Father's name."	John v. 43. "Comes in his own."
Phil. ii. 8. " Humbled himself and became obedient."	2. Thess. ii. 4. " Exalts himself above all."
Is. liii. 3. " Was despised and rejected and we esteemed him not."	Rev. xiii. 3, 4. " All the world wonder after the beast, saying, who is like unto him ?"
John vi. 38. " Comes to do his Father's will."	Daniel xi. 31. " Does according to his own."
John xvii. 4. " Glorifies God on earth."	Rev. xiii. 6. " Blasphemes the name of God."
John x. 14, 15. "The good Shepherd that giveth his life for the sheep."	Zech. xi. 16, 17. " The evil shepherd or idol shepherd who shall tear the flesh."
Phil. ii. 9, 10. " God highly exalts him, and gives him a name above every name, that at the name of Jesus every knee should bow."	Is. xiv. 14, 15. " Exalteth himself above the heights of the clouds, yet is brought down to hell."
Matt. xxiv. 30. " Shall be seen coming in the clouds with power and great glory."	Is. xiv. 16. " They that see thee shall narrowly look upon thee, saying, Is this the man that made the earth to tremble, that did shake the kingdoms ? "
Rev. xi. 15. " Shall reign for ever and ever."	Dan. vii. 26. " They shall take away his dominion to consume and destroy it to the end."
Heb. i. 2. " The heir of all things."	2 Thess. ii. 3. " The son of perdition."

Although we might dwell, at length, upon the texts thus cited and compared, as furnishing clear and substantial criteria, by which to recognize and identify Antichrist when he shall enter upon his career, and by which to determine many of his principal characteristics, and many of the principal incidents of his reign, yet our only object now is to refer to them, as establishing, beyond a question, his *personality*. If on the other hand, they afford no evidence of his personality, then do not the contrasted texts, on the other, afford any evidence of the personality of Christ. If we claim that the one class of texts fail to prove the personality of Antichrist, of one particular Antichrist, as contradistinguished from and preëminent over all types and forerunners which shall have preceded him, then, upon the same principles of logic and evidence by which this conclusion is reached, must the other class of texts equally fail to prove the personality of Christ. Deny that the prophets, Old and New Testament alike, prove the existence of THE particular, personal and final Antichrist, or that they describe the principal events of his career, and it is impossible, in all logical fairness, not to deny, also, that the prophets and evangelists prove the existence of THE particular and personal Christ (as distinguished, if you please, from the " false Christs," which he warned his disciples would come in his name), and that they record the principal acts of his life and the principal events of his career.

True, the prophet who portrays the beast of the Revelation elsewhere informs us that there are many antichrists (1 John ii. 18), indeed, that whosoever denies that Christ *is to come* (ἐρχόμενον in the original, and *venturus* in the Vulgate) in the flesh is antichrist; but it will be observed that he does not, in his epistle, as in the Revelation, call these antichrists by name, or give us any particular account of them, or attach any specific title to them. It is of antichristianism, of the "spirit of antichrist," of which the prophet, *professedly*, discourses in his epistle, but it is of THE Antichrist that he discourses, and whose portraiture he draws, in the Revelation; not of his types and forerunners of any or of all ages, of Antiochus Epiphanes, or Mohammed, or the Napoleons, or either of them, or any one Pope, or any succession of Popes, however signally they may have foreshadowed his reign, or contributed to cast up a highway for him; but of the literal Antichrist of the very last days, of, so to speak, the very *closing hours* of the Gentile dispensation; of the great *final* monarch of the prophetic earth, and of him alone. The prophet of the Revelation means, as Daniel, the great apocalyptic revelator of the Old Testament, meant before him, that there should be no mistake as to the personal identity, or the lofty preëminence in evil, of *this last* Antichrist, or as to the distinctive and expressly revealed characteristics of his reign.

To further illustrate the personal identity of this literal and final Antichrist, but, more especially, to identify the symbols enumerated at the commencement of this chapter, as referring, one and all, to one and the same person, we will compare the accounts given of him under these symbols in different chapters of Daniel and the Revelation, premising only that we can but anticipate the surprise of the reader (once having made himself familiar with the portraiture of Antichrist in the Revelation) to find how easily he will be able to follow him, under every change of symbol, under every altered title, through, not the pages of Daniel only, but the entire range of prophetic Scripture, never, for a moment losing sight of him, or erring as to his personal identity in all its strict and proper fulness. Thus;

AS THE BEAST.	AS THE LITTLE HORN.
Rev. xiii. 6. "He opens his mouth in blasphemy against God, to blaspheme his name, and his tabernacle, and them that dwell in heaven."	Dan. vii. 25. "He speaks great words against the Most High."
Rev. xiii. 7. "He makes war with the saints and overcomes them."	Dan. vii. 21. "He makes war with the saints and prevails."
Rev. xiii. 5. "Authority was given unto him forty and two months," i. e. 1260 days.	Dan. vii. 25. "The saints are given into his hand until time, times and the dividing of time," i. e. 1260 days.

A strong presumption certainly that the beast of the thirteenth of the Revelation and the little horn of the seventh of Daniel are identical, symbols of one and the same person. Again;

AS THE LITTLE HORN.	AS THE SECOND LITTLE HORN.
Dan. vii. 25. "Speaks great words against the Most High."	Dan. xi. 36. "Speaks marvellous things against the God of gods."
Dan. vii. 22. "Shall prevail until the Ancient of days comes, and judgment is given to the saints of the Most High, and the time comes that the saints possess the kingdom."	Dan. xi. 36. Shall prosper till the indignation [against Israel and Jerusalem] be accomplished."

Thus the symbols of the seventh and eleventh of Daniel are as clearly identical as those of the seventh of Daniel and the thirteenth of the Revelation. Again;

AS THE SECOND LITTLE HORN.	AS THE KING OF FIERCE COUNTENANCE.
Dan. xi. 41. "He shall enter also into the glorious land."	Dan. viii. 9. "He waxes great towards the pleasant land."
Dan. xi. 40. "Enters the glorious land at the time of the end."	Dan. viii. 17. "At the time of the end shall be the vision."
Dan. xi. 36. "He shall prosper till the indignation [against Israel and Jerusalem] be accomplished."	Dan. viii. 19. "He shall prosper in the last end of the indignation" [against Israel and Jerusalem].

Thus the identity of the king of fierce countenance of the eighth and the little horn of the eleventh of Daniel can not be denied, as it appears to us, without, at the same time, denying the identity of the symbols previously considered, and their identity one and all with that of the eighth of Daniel. Finally;

THE KING OF FIERCE COUN-TENANCE.	THE PRINCE THAT SHALL COME.
Dan. viii. 11. "Takes away the daily sacrifice."	Dan. ix. 27. "Causes the sacrifice and oblation to cease."
Dan. viii. 19. "Shall prosper in the last end of the indignation."	Dan. ix. 27. "Till that determined is poured upon the desolator."

Thus are the beast of the thirteenth of the Revelation, the little horn of the seventh, the little horn of the eleventh, the king of fierce countenance of the eighth, and the prince that shall come of the ninth, of Daniel, identical symbols, representative of the literal and final Antichrist of prophecy. We say *final*, because it will be observed that, with a single exception, the last two contrasted texts in each of the foregoing sets of comparisons, establish his fall as being "when the indignation [against Israel and Jerusalem] shall be accomplished," which, certainly, as the observation of the most indifferent must convince them, has not been accomplished as yet, and as being "at the time of the end," which has certainly not yet arrived.

The evidence by which the identity of the symbols, thus variously and concurrently representing Antichrist in prophetic Scripture is clearly established, might be multiplied indefinitely. We add a single instance more. "The prince that shall come" of the ninth of Daniel, "shall prosper until the consummation, and that determined is poured upon the desolator." (v. 27.) The "king of Assyria" of the tenth of Isaiah shall prosper "till the Lord hath performed his whole work upon Mount Zion, and on Jerusalem." The "king of Assyria" is, therefore, still another title of the Antichrist.

In the fourteenth of Isaiah he is again called the Assyrian, "The Lord of hosts hath sworn, saying, Surely as I have thought, so shall it come to pass; and as I have purposed, so shall it stand: That I will break the Assyrian *in my land*, and upon my mountains tread him under foot; THEN shall his yoke depart from off them and his burden from off their shoulders"—i. e. *the shoulders of Israel;* a sure proof of their restoration in unbelief.

In the same chapter he is also called "the king of Babylon" and "Lucifer," from his blasphemous assumption, perhaps, of the character of Christ as the bright and morning star.

We have thus considered some of the evidences of the personality of the literal and final Antichrist of prophecy, and of the identity of not a few of the various symbols by which he is represented; which evidences contain, in most instances, direct proof, and, in all, conclusive implications, of the futurity of his reign.

It remains to consider, more particularly and more by themselves, still other proofs of the *futurity* of the reign of Antichrist, though nothing, probably, could establish that fact more completely than the plain declarations of prophetic Scripture already considered, which place the period of his reign "at the time of the end"; when "the indignation [against Israel and Jerusalem] shall be accomplished"; "when the Lord hath performed his whole work upon Mount Zion, and on Jerusalem"; in "the last end of the indignation"—and "when the transgressors are come to the full," i. e. when their full number is accomplished, which certainly is not as yet. These plain declarations are perfectly definite and conclusive, and yet they are but a tithe of the scriptural evidence of the futurity of Antichrist's reign, nor do we propose, in proceeding to the consideration of further proof on this point, to allude to more than a tithe of that which remains.

First, Antichrist is described as "exalting himself above all that is called God, or that is worshipped," 2 Thess. ii. 4; as "planting the tabernacles of his palace between the seas [the Dead and Mediterranean] in the glorious holy mountain," Daniel xi. 45; as *sitting in the temple of God, shewing himself that he is God.*"—2 Thess. ii. 4.

Now "the temple of God" is an expression applied in Scripture to three things, and three only; 1st. To the actual temple at Jerusalem, as in 1 Sam. i. 9. 2d. To the bodies of individual saints, as in 1 Cor. vi. 19. 3d. To the Church of God, as in 1 Cor. iii. 17. It is manifestly impossible that Antichrist could sit in any but the first of these three, and the co-inciding expression of Daniel, "the glorious holy mountain," fixes the locality of that temple, not, as some would have it, at Rome, but in the holy city, at Jerusalem and there only.

We have seen that the symbols of Antichrist in Daniel and the symbol of Antichrist in the Revelation are identical, also that the periods at which these prophets severally predicted his reign, are identical. Their descriptions in this regard are perfectly precise and harmonious.

But the Apocalypse was written by John *twenty years* after the destruction of Jerusalem by Titus, A. D. 71, and was a revelation, as the term itself implies, not of the *past*, but of the *future*. But there has been no temple at Jerusalem thus to "sit in" and to pollute, from the time of its destruction by Titus even until now. John, therefore (and not less Daniel), in prophetically recording the desecration of the Jewish temple by Antichrist, must have had reference to a period which is clearly and unquestionably *future*.

And here, in passing, we pause for a moment, to show, more specifically, that Antiochus Epiphanes, could not, as many have supposed, have been the Antichrist either of Daniel or the Revelation (although Daniel, in his eleventh chapter, describes Antiochus at length as polluting the Jewish temple and worship), for he died *more than one hundred and sixty years before Christ*. He can not, therefore, be the Antichrist of John, and if not of John certainly not of Daniel, for we have seen that they are identical. Antiochus is, perhaps, the most remarkable of all the types of Antichrist, certainly in many respects. He overrun the holy city and the holy land. He "took away the daily sacrifice." He profaned the temple. But he did not live "at the time of the end," "in the last end of the indignation," "when the transgressors were come to the full," when the Lord had "performed his whole work upon Mount Zion, and on Jerusalem." He did not "stand up against the Prince of princes." He was not "broken without hand," i. e. by special and direct divine interposition. He did not reign in undivided sovereignty over the ten prophetic realms of the eastern and western Roman earth, nor did any ten confederated kings therein flee to him, to seek, under his more iron rule, a refuge from the popular commotions that menaced their thrones. The age of democracy, of the struggle for independence of the clay, as against the iron, was comparatively unknown and undeveloped then. For the same reason Mohammed can not have been Antichrist, nor can any Pope, nor any number or succession of Popes. There is, moreover, no mountain in Rome, much less the " glorious holy mountain " of which Daniel speaks, and to which our Saviour alludes, as he does in the twenty-fourth of Matthew, as the seat of the " Holy Place." There are not (as we have shown) seven distinct hills even there. There is no Temple of God there, capable of being thus desecrated and profaned, unless it be claimed that it is St. Peter's, which, surely, with its satanic record, is any thing, and has ever been any thing, rather than " THE Holy Place." Certainly Bishop Colenso could not, by any possible ingenuity of his " verifying faculty," or in any possible consistency with his neologic conceits, so contract the range of his Anglican latitudinarianism, as to grant to the Pope so full and exclusive a dispensation as this. Not thus does he minister at the altars of symbolic Babylon!

Again; we are told by Daniel that the period of Antichrist's reign will be a season of unexampled tribulation. He says, expressly, that this tribulation will be " at the time of the end," and that it will be connected immediately with the reign of Antichrist.

" And he [Antichrist] shall plant the tabernacles of his palace between the seas in the glorious holy mountain

".... and *at that time* there shall be a time of trouble, such as never was since there was a nation, . . . and at this time thy people [the House of Israel] shall be delivered, every one that shall be found written in the book."
—Daniel xi. 45 ; xii. 1.

John, in the Revelation, refers distinctly to the severity of this tribulation, identifying it plainly with the reign of Antichrist.

" And it was given unto him [the beast] to make war with the saints, and to overcome them . . . . and he causeth all, the small and the great, and the rich and the poor, and the free and the bond, to receive a mark on their right hand, or on their forehead : [and] that no one be able to buy or to sell, save he that hath the mark, the name of the beast, or the number of his name . . . . . and all that dwell upon the earth shall worship him, whose names are not written in the book of life of the Lamb slain from the foundation of the world."—Revelation xiii.

So also our Saviour foretold this season of tribulation to his disciples, connecting it immediately with the reign of Antichrist, and his own second appearing.

" When ye therefore shall see the abomination of desolation, spoken of by Daniel the prophet, stand in the holy place . . . . . there shall be great tribulation, such as was not since the beginning of the world to this time, no, nor ever shall be. . . . . *Immediately after* the tribulation of those days shall the sun be darkened, and the moon shall not give her light, and the stars shall fall from heaven, and the powers of the heavens shall be shaken ; and then shall appear the sign of the Son of man in heaven, and then shall all the tribes of the earth mourn, and they shall see the Son of man coming in the clouds of heaven with power and great glory."—Matthew xxiv.

Now if this season of unprecedented and unexampled tribulation has already past, then is "the time of the end" also past; then, also, has Antichrist "planted the tabernacles of his palace between the seas in the glorious holy mountain" in the past; then has the full number of transgressors been accomplished in the past; then has the indignation against Israel and Jerusalem ceased, and the House of Israel been delivered, in the past; then has the sign of the Son of man, which our Saviour foretold, (*not reverted to*) appeared in heaven in the past; then has the Son of man come again in his own glory, and in his Father's glory, and in the glory of the holy angels, and the righteous living been transformed, and the sainted dead been raised from their graves, in the past, to meet him at his coming; then are we living in the millennium now. Alas, how many aching hearts, and weary heads, and weeping eyes, how many righteous and believing souls, will attest the contrary! If, therefore, we are not living in the millennium now, and Antichrist is not reigning now, as we know from indubitable criteria (already referred to) that he is not, then must his reign, clearly and unquestionably, be *future*.

Once more; not only is the empire of Antichrist (embracing the territory comprised within the boundaries of the four great world powers, as already considered) to be supernaturally destroyed "at the time of the end," and "in the days of these kings" (the ten kings of the prophetic earth, Daniel ii. 44) by the "stone cut out of the mountain, without hands," but Antichrist is, at the same time, to be *supernaturally destroyed himself*. We cite the following Scripture in proof.

"He shall also stand up against the Prince of princes, but he shall be destroyed without hand," (Daniel viii. 25) i. e., by direct divine interposition, which interposition, it is worthy of notice, will be attended with various miraculous signs and tokens, such as are described by our Saviour,—the darkening of the sun, the witholding of the light of the moon, the falling of the stars from heaven, and the shaking of its powers.

"These [the ten kings of the prophetic earth and the beast] shall make war upon the Lamb and the Lamb shall overcome them, for he is the Lord of lords and the King of kings."—Revelation xvii. 12, 14.

"And I saw the beast and the kings of the earth, and his armies, gathered together to make war upon him that sat on the horse, and with his army [the legions of heaven.] And the beast was taken, and he who was with him, the false prophet, that wrought miracles in his presence, with which he deceived those that received the mark of the beast, and those that worship his image. [What false prophet thus ministers, or has ever thus ministered, to the Pope of Rome?) These both were cast alive into the lake of fire which burneth with brimstone. And the rest were killed with the sword of him that sat upon the horse, which sword proceeded out of his mouth; and all the fowls were filled with their flesh."—Rev. xix. 19—21.

So also the apostle Paul expressly couples the supernatural destruction of Antichrist with Christ's second coming.

"The man of sin, the son of perdition . . that wicked one whom the Lord shall consume with the breath of his spirit, and destroy with the brightness of his coming."— 2 Thes. ii. 3, 8.

So also Isaiah;

"And he shall smite the earth with the rod of his mouth, and with the breath of his lips shall he slay the wicked one."—xi. 4.

In the light of this Scripture, it is enough simply to ask what sovereign of the entire (eastern and western) prophetic earth, holding sway over its ten allied realms and ten concurring kings, has ever been thus supernaturally destroyed in the past? If no one, then must the reign of Antichrist be, most clearly and unquestionably, *future*.

We have thus considered the *personality* of Antichrist; the *identity of the symbols which represent him;* the *sphere*, in its precise boundaries, and the *futurity*, in its appointed period, of his reign. Let us now consider, more particularly, the *prophetic record* of his reign.

Its most distinguishing feature will be its connection with Israel and Jerusalem. In this connection, it would almost appear as if Antichrist were to be raised up purposely to be the judicial, final and most consuming scourge of God's "chosen people." His record, in this regard, is to be found, chiefly, in the last six chapters of Daniel. The first six chapters give us a picture of the four great Gentile empires, and the course of Gentile civilization from its commencement to its close; the last six a picture of Israel and Jerusalem as affected by Gentile rule and the reign of Antichrist. The first six revolve around Babylon as their centre; the last six around Jerusalem. The first six are written in the native tongue of Babylon, the Chaldee; the last six in the native tongue of Israel, the

Hebrew. The first six give us, in outline, the career of the great Gentile kings who precede Antichrist; the last six give us, in detail, the principal acts of Antichrist as connected with Israel and Jerusalem. It is thus, and thus only, that it is possible to view Antichrist in proper boldness of relief. Israel and Jerusalem, far more than many would at first suppose, constitute the great key-note of human history, and Antichrist will, on the one hand, be their last, their most vengeful, and, for a season, their most successful foe, as he will be, on the other, the last great idol of Gentile civilization, the representative of its grandest epoch, "wondered after and worshipped by all." But the Jews are to be "trodden under foot of the Gentiles" to the very end.

Contemporaneously with his reign, the Jews will be a restored, but still unforgiven and unbelieving nation, with a rebuilded temple and reinstituted worship. Their worldly resources and worldly pride will be beyond all precedent or comparison. This is the special burden of the second chapter of Isaiah. "Replenished from the East, their land will be full of silver and gold, neither is there any end of their treasures; their land is also full of horses, neither is there any end of their chariots; their land is also full of idols."—Isaiah ii. 6—8. Thus, though restored as a nation, they will be restored, not in favor, but in anger. Judgments more consuming than were ever inflicted upon them before await them now. "The Lord shall lop their bough with terror, and the high ones of stature shall be hewn down, and the haughty shall be made humble." Antichrist will be the instrument employed. " I will send him against an hypocritical nation, and against the people of my wrath will I give him a charge, to take the spoil, and to take the prey, and to tread them down like the mire of the streets." (Isaiah x. 9.) " Wherefore thus saith the Lord God; Because ye are all become dross, behold, therefore I will bring you [the entire House of Israel, *all* the tribes] into the midst of Jerusalem. As they gather silver, and brass, and iron, and lead, and tin, into the midst of the furnace, to blow upon it, to melt it; so will I gather you [when have they ever been so gathered in the past?] in my anger and my fury, and I will leave you there and melt you. Yes! I will gather you, and blow upon you in the fire of my wrath, and ye shall be melted in the midst thereof; and ye shall know that I the Lord have poured out my fury upon you."—Ezekiel xxii. 19—22.

"And the people of the prince that shall come shall destroy the city, and the sanctuary; and the end thereof shall be with a flood, and unto the end of the war [of Antichrist against Israel and Jerusalem] desolations are determined."—Daniel ix. 26.

These persecutions will not cease until the hour for the destruction of Antichrist, and the co-incident conversion of Israel shall arrive.

If the Jews are to be restored as a believing and forgiven nation, as some believe, why these persecutions after their return? If they are to be converted *as a nation*, as we know from Zechariah that they are to be, then, of course, must they have returned unconverted.

The Jews will, at first, willingly receive Antichrist. " I am come in my Father's name and ye receive me not, if another shall come in his own name, him ye will receive."

Antichrist will enter into a covenant with them,

"cleaving unto them with flatteries." "And he shall confirm the covenant with many [i. e., with Israel] for one week [or hebdomad, a period of seven years], and in the midst of the week [at the end of three and a half years] he shall cause the sacrifice and the oblation to cease, and for the overspreading of abominations he shall make it desolate, even until the consummation and that determined shall be poured upon the desolator." (Daniel ix. 27.) That is, in his jealousy of the undivided homage and worship of all adherents of his dominion, and of every vestige and memorial, however prostituted, of the true God, he will violate his covenant, assail Jerusalem, and make war upon its people. He will, for a time, be victorious. He will overthrow the Jewish worship. He will "plant the tabernacles of his palace between the seas in the glorious holy mountain." He will "sit in the temple of God, showing himself that he is God," "exalting himself above all that is called God, or that is worshipped," setting up "the abomination of desolation" in the "Holy Place." Then shall there be a time of trouble for Israel, such as shall not have been since there was a nation, no, nor ever shall be. "Behold the day [not the "day of the Lord," of Christ's second coming; that is still future] cometh for Jehovah, and thy spoil shall be divided in the midst of thee. For I will gather all nations against Jerusalem to battle; and the city shall be taken, and the houses rifled, and the women ravished; and half of the city shall go forth into captivity, and the residue of the people shall not be cut off." (Zechariah xiv. 2.) This description applies, in no sense, to the subsequent and final siege of Jerusalem, for then the city will not be taken, no outrage will be committed upon it by its foes, no portion of it will go forth into captivity.

But the end draweth nigh. "For the elects' sake [now so nearly worn out by Antichrist] those days shall be shortened." Antichrist "shall come to his end and none shall help him." The "battle of the great day of God the Almighty" is at hand. But Antichrist little foresees that he will be opposed by the armies of heaven and their divine Commander, APPEARING IN PROPER PERSON.

For some untold reason, the "residue that is not cut off" rebel again against the rule of Antichrist and defy his utmost rage. Whereupon he prepares to assail Jerusalem more fiercely than ever.

"For behold, in those days, and in that time, when I shall bring again the captivity of Judah and Jerusalem, I will also gather all nations [of the prophetic earth] and will bring them down into the valley of Jehoshaphat [Jehovah judging] and will plead with them for my people, and for my heritage Israel, whom they have scattered among the nations, and parted my land."—Joel iii. 1, 2.

"Proclaim ye this among the Gentiles: Prepare war, wake up the mighty men, let all the men of war draw near, let them come up: Beat your ploughshares into swords, your pruning hooks into spears. . . . . Put ye in the sickle, for the harvest is ripe; come, and get ye down, for the press is full, the vats overflow; for their wickedness is great. Multitudes, multitudes in the valley of decision. . . . . The Lord also shall roar out of Zion, and utter his voice from Jerusalem, and the heavens and the earth shall shake, but the Lord will be the hope of his people, and the strength of the children of Israel."—Joel iii. 9—16.

"The Lord shall go forth, and fight against those nations, as when he fought in the day of battle, and *his feet shall stand in that day upon the Mount of Olives.*"—Zechariah xiv. 3, 4.

"And it shall come to pass in that day, that I will seek to destroy [not *all* nations, but] all the nations that come against Jerusalem [i. e., the ten nations of the prophetic earth] . . . and they [i. e., Israel] *shall look upon me whom they have pierced*, and they shall mourn for him, as one mourneth for his only son."—Zechariah xii. 9, 10.

"And when they had spoken these things, while they beheld, he was taken up; and a cloud received him out of their sight. And while they looked steadfastly towards heaven as he went up, behold, two men stood by them in white apparel; which also said, Ye men of Galilee, why stand ye gazing up into heaven? *this same Jesus that is taken up from you into heaven, shall so come in like manner as ye have seen him go into heaven.*"—Acts i. 9—11.

"And they shall see the Son of man coming in the clouds of heaven with power and great glory."—Our Saviour, in Matthew xxiv. 30.

"For they are the spirits of demons, working miracles, that go forth unto the kings of the whole world [τῆς οἰκουμένης ὅλης, i. e., the whole prophetic earth,] to gather them to the battle of the great day of God the Almighty. . . . . And they gathered them together into the place which is called in Hebrew Armageddon. . . . . . These [i. e., the ten kings of the prophetic earth, *and the beast*] shall make war upon the Lamb, and the Lamb shall overcome them, because he is the Lord of lords, and King of kings, and those who are with him are called, and chosen, and faithful." . . . . "And I saw heaven opened, and

behold a white horse; and he that sat upon him was [called] Faithful and True. . . . . And the armies which were in heaven were following him . . . and out of his mouth proceeded a sharp sword, that with it he should smite the nations: and he shall rule them with a rod of iron: and he treadeth the winepress of the fierceness of the wrath of God the Almighty. And he hath on his garment and on his thigh a name written, KING OF KINGS, AND LORD OF LORDS. And I saw an angel standing in the sun; and he cried with a loud voice, saying to all the fowls that fly in the mid-heaven, Come, be gathered together unto the great supper of God; that ye may eat the flesh of kings, and the flesh of chief-captains, and the flesh of mighty men, and the flesh of horses, and of those that sit on them, and the flesh of all men, both small and great. And I saw the beast, and the kings of the earth, and his armies, gathered together to make war with him that sat on the horse, and with his army. And the beast was taken, and he who was with him, the false prophet that wrought miracles in his presence, with which he deceived those that worship his image. These both were cast alive into the lake of fire which burneth with brimstone. And the rest were killed with the sword of him that sat upon the horse, which sword proceeded out of his mouth: and all the fowls were filled with their flesh."
—Revelation xvi., xvii., xix.*

But Antichrist and his armies are not to be the only

---

* This will not be the only occasion when there has been a direct and visible interference of almighty power for the deliverance of Israel. God divided the Red Sea for their escape from Egypt. He caused the walls of Jericho to fall down. He fought for them against the kings of Canaan He descended on Sinai to confirm with them, for their future guidance, the covenant of the Law with its glorious but rejected alternative of perpetual blessing. Sinai trembled and was shaken; and He has said, " Yet one more I shake not the earth only, but also heaven."

victims of the interposing vengeance of heaven. The hour of the final destruction of his golden capital, the literal Babylon of prophecy, has also arrived. Note the call that summons forth the hordes of central and northern Asia to its destruction, even while his armies are beleaguring Jerusalem.

"Set ye up a standard in the land, blow the trumpet among the nations, prepare the nations against her, the kingdoms of Ararat, Minni and Aschenaz, appoint a captain against her; cause the horses to come up as the rough caterpillars. Prepare against her the nations with the kings of the Medes, the captains thereof, and all the rulers thereof. And the land [of Babylon] shall tremble and sorrow: for every purpose of the Lord shall be performed against Babylon, to make her a desolation without an inhabitant."—Jeremiah 1. 27—29.*

Thus Babylon will fall. Thus "her broad walls shall be broken, and her high gates be burned with fire," "her mighty men be taken, and every one of their bows be broken," "for the spoilers have come unto her from the north," even at the very time (as swift messengers from Babylon will hasten to announce) that the Lord of hosts "shall break the Assyrian in his land," and "upon His mountains tread him under foot." Israel, now repentant and forgiven, will rejoice and lift up her loud and triumphant acclaim, "How hath the oppressor ceased—the golden city ceased."

Thus sets, in divided glory and gloom, the Saturday evening's sun of this Gentile dispensation, briefly pre-

---

* The "nations" here referred to can not be the same as those described as being gathered, under Antichrist, before Jerusalem, for the latter are said expressly to be those of the ten kings of the prophetic earth. See Revelation xvii. 12, 13, 14.

ceding the millennial dawn of the new Judaic dispensation, when Jerusalem shall, at last, " dwell safely," at rest from her Gentile foes ; when " her light shall go forth as brightness, and the salvation thereof as a lamp that burneth " to " all the families of the earth," with none to molest or make afraid in all God's holy mountain. Thus, too, shall Antichrist arise and " prosper and practice " and pass away, and the groaning and travailing earth, now, at last, relieved, enter upon a Sabbath of peaceful and blessed rest, and Satan be bound for a thousand years.

Oh, how boundless, as a source of comfort and support and repose, will be the prospect of that millennial rest, with its earthly felicity and its heavenly ministrations, to those destined to pass through the perilous scenes of the great tribulation, upon the very threshold of which we are entering even now! Verily, on the other side of that fiery flood, there is " a rest that remaineth to the people of God," where all tears will be wiped away and there will be no cross to bear. Earth hath no sorrow which that rest will not heal.

CHAPTER V.

ISRAEL AND JERUSALEM OF PROPHECY.

GOD'S COVENANTS CONCERNING THEM, AND THEIR FINAL EXALTATION.

INTIMATELY connected with the subjects of the preceding chapters — the restoration of the Jews, *as an undivided and incorporated nation*, to their own land — their restoration *in unbelief*—their *subsequent persecutions under Antichrist*, and their final *forgiveness and blessing*— are God's covenants concerning them, and concerning his and their "beloved city."

These covenants consist of a regular series, and bind up within themselves almost the entire history of the Jewish nation, insomuch that their history can not be properly understood without properly understanding these covenants also.

They are four in number, the Abrahamic, the Mosaic, the Davidic, and the "new and everlasting covenant of grace."

We shall consider them in the order in which Scripture places them, that is, in the order of time.

First in order, both in importance and in time, is the Abrahamic covenant.

Concerning this covenant it should be said, before entering upon a more particular consideration of it, that, perhaps, there is no higher scriptural evidence of the future restoration of both families of the House of Israel, as an undivided nation, to their own land, and of the restoration of the land itself to more than its ancient beauty, fertility and glory, than the very terms in which this covenant is, not only at first expressed, but afterwards so fully and repeatedly confirmed. This covenant is not only the proper and essential starting point, but the very key to a just biblical understanding of the past and present suffering condition, and the final earthly glory of Israel and Jerusalem.

Abraham, obedient to the command of God, "left his country, his kindred and his father's house," and journeyed westward toward Canaan. Having entered Canaan, not knowing whither he was to go, or where he was to take up even a temporary abode, he continued his journey until he reached the plain of Moreh. There "the Lord appeared unto him and said, *Unto thy seed will I give this land.*" And Abraham built an altar there unto the Lord.

Subsequently, after his return from Egypt, he came again unto "the place where his tent had been pitched at the beginning, unto the place of the altar which he had made there at the first." The Lord, appearing to him, not directly upon the plain of Moreh, but upon a not distant mountain, from whence the land, afterwards called Holy, stretched on every side, to its farthest extent of view, "said unto Abraham, *Lift up now thine eyes, and look from the place where thou art, northward, and southward, and eastward, and westward: for all the land which thou seest, to thee will I give it, and to thy seed for ever. Arise, walk through the land, in the length of it, and in the breadth of it; for I will give it unto thee.*" From this elevated site, in the clear atmosphere of Canaan, the patriarch could not see a single spot, in the entire range of view that encircled him, except the peak of a far distant mountain, that did not form a portion of the land given by these words of the Lord to him and to his seed for ever. Verily, " a good land and a large," a gift worthy, in its freeness, and fulness, and richness, and perpetuity, of the Lord of the whole earth to give to Abraham, his servant and his friend!

This gift the Lord afterwards confirmed by a covenant, defining more particularly its extent, on the day when he announced to the aged and childless pilgrim that he would give unto him a son (to be the " heir no less of the spiritual than material blessings promised unto him). " In the same day the Lord made a covenant with Abraham, saying, *Unto thy seed have I given this land, from the river of Egypt unto the great river, the river Euphrates; the Kenites, and the Kennizzites, and the Kadmonites, and the Hittites, and the Perizzites, and the Rephaims, and the Amorites, and the Canaanites, and the Girgashites, and the Jebusites.*"

Again; in visions of the night, "the Lord called him forth from the curtains of his tent and commanded him, " *Look now towards heaven, and tell the stars, if thou be able to number them.*" Under the pure skies of a Judean night, he lifted up his eyes to the innumerable heavenly host, " and the word of the Lord said unto him, *So shall thy seed be, I am the Lord that brought thee out of Ur of the Chaldees, to give thee this land to inherit it.*"

Finally; when Abraham was ninety years old and nine, and one year before the birth of Isaac, the Lord again appeared to him and said, "*I will establish my covenant between me and thee and thy seed after thee, in their generations, for an everlasting covenant, to be a God unto thee, and to thy seed after thee. And I will give unto thee and to thy seed after thee, the land wherein thou art a stranger, all the land of Canaan, for an everlasting possession; and I will be their God.*" Verily, a gift of godlike munificence to one, who, previously thereto, was neither the father of an heir, nor, humanly speaking, likely to be, nor the owner of a foot of ground! But he trusted in the most High God, the possessor of heaven and earth, and kept his charge, his commandments, his statutes, and his laws. This was the secret of the promise and the blessing.

If the plainest of terms and the divinest of authority can establish the right of the seed of Abraham to the possession of the land of promise, against the adverse claims or occupancy of any and all other nations; or the everlasting tenure of that right; or the certainty that it will be ultimately and nationally enjoyed as an everlasting inheritance; then, surely, such right, with all the privileges and blessings pertaining to it, is granted here. No intervals of interrupted possession, or dispersion and persecution in other lands, no tenancy of other nations, of whatever duration, can devest a right, or impair the certainty of its ultimate and everlasting enjoyment, clothed with sanctions so sacred. No human proscription, no technical forfeiture, can run against so divine a title.

Observe now, briefly, the renewals by the Almighty of this covenant.

To Isaac, God said, "*Sojourn in this land, and I will be with thee and bless thee ; for unto thee and thy seed will*

I give all these countries; and I will perform the oath which I sware unto Abraham thy father, and I will make thy seed to multiply as the stars of heaven, and will give unto thy seed all these countries; and in thy seed shall all the nations of the earth be blessed."

To Jacob, God said, " *The land which I gave Abraham and Isaac, to thee will I give it, and to thy seed after thee will I give the land.*"

The dying Joseph said to his brethren in Egypt, " God will surely bring you out of this land unto the land which he sware to Abraham and Isaac and Jacob."

Such is the Abrahamic covenant; such the circumstances under which it was made; the terms in which it is expressed; the divinely official sanctions which invest it; its renewals, and its perpetuity; such the title it conveys, and the muniments by which that title is surrounded. Such is the heaven-chartered right, which Antichrist will seek, with unprecedented fury, to wrest from this now dispersed and despised and bleeding people, and such the covenants and oaths by which the God of Israel will oppose the fierce onsets of his Satanic wrath.

The territory thus granted [not to *all* the seed of Abraham and Isaac, for they had other seed than Jacob, to whom these covenants did not pertain, and who had no inheritance in Israel, but to *all the seed of Jacob*] was not left by the Almighty uncertain or undefined. Its exact boundaries, at all points, are laid down in Scripture, with the most careful and unambiguous precision, whatever difficulty there may be in defining them with similar accuracy in modern terms.

When the Lord appeared unto Moses with the declared

purpose of delivering the children of Israel from their Egyptian captivity, and of thus fulfilling his covenants with Abraham and Isaac and Jacob, he said, " I am come down to deliver my people — and to bring them up out of the land of Egypt, and to bring them unto a good land and a large." God himself defined the limits of the land, " And I will set thy bounds by the Red Sea, even unto the sea of the Philistines, and from the desert unto the river. .... Every place whereon the soles of your feet shall tread shall be yours; from the wilderness and Lebanon, from the river, the river Euphrates, even unto the uttermost sea shall your coast be."—Deut. xi. 22—26.

Again, Moses defines, as follows, a portion of its borders, in the thirty-fourth chapter of Numbers (6—11.) "As for the western border, ye shall have the great sea for a border; this shall be your west border. This shall be your north border; from the great sea ye shall point out for you Mount Hor. From Mount Hor ye shall point out your border unto the entrance of Hamath; and the goings forth of the border shall be to Zedad. And the border shall go on to Ziphron, and the goings out of it shall be at Hazar-enan; this shall be your north border. And ye shall point out your east border from Hazar-enan to Shepham; and the coast shall go down from Shepham to Riblah, on the east side Ain," &c.

Thus, as above, has Moses recorded the limits of the Promised Land, after the Canaanitish tribes had acquired a prescriptive right thereto (if such a thing were possible against the sure word of God) by adverse and uninterrupted possession during a period of four hundred years.

Centuries afterwards, when all the tribes of Israel were captive bondmen in lands far distant from Jerusalem and Samaria, a portion of them for a period of seventy years, but by far the greater portion for a period which has not ended even now, the prophet Ezekiel, himself a fellow-exile in Chaldea with Daniel and Jeremiah and the tribes of Judah and Benjamin, thus, as follows, defines, in perfect harmony with Moses, the boundaries of the Promised Land, and declares to the sorrowing and weeping exiles by the waters of Babylon, not less, than its divinely appointed borders, the immutability of God's covenants concerning it:

"Thus saith the Lord God, This shall be the border whereby ye shall inherit the land according to the twelve tribes of Israel; Joseph shall have two portions. And ye shall inherit it one as well as another; *concerning the which I lifted up my hand to give it unto your fathers;* and this land shall fall to you for inheritance. And this shall be the border of the land toward the north side, from the great sea, the way of Hethlon, as men go to Zedad; Hamath, Berothah, Sibraim, which is between the border of Damascus and the border of Hamath; Hazar-hatticon, which is by the coast of Hauran. And the border from the sea shall be Hazar-enan, the border of Damascus, and the north northward, and the border of Hamath. And this is the north side. And the east side ye shall measure from Hauran, and from Damascus, and from Gilead, and from the land of Israel by Jordan, from the border unto the east sea. And this is the east side. And the south side southward, from Tamar to the waters of strife in Kadesh, the river to the great sea. And this is the south side southward. The west side also shall be the great sea from the border, till a man comes over against Hamath. This is the west side. So shall ye divide this land according to the tribes of Israel."—Ezekiel xlvii. 13—22.

We may not be able to trace these boundaries now as accurately as the above description would seem to imply, or to verify them in terms of modern geography, but they are not, for that reason, any the less absolutely definite, as the immutable and divinely-declared limits of the Promised Land; as immutable to-day as on those far distant days, when God, both by direct communication, and by the mouth of his holy prophets, first defined them. And the immutability of his covenanted purposes concerning the children of Israel and their land can no more be shaken by any occupancy, or user, or prescriptive claims of other nations, during these long and weary centuries of dispersion and persecution among the Gentiles, than it was by the captivity of four hundred years in Egypt, or the exile of seventy years at Babylon. *All the tribes* will, as truly as God liveth, and his covenant standeth sure, go back to the Promised Land from their Gentile dispersion, even as all went back from their Egyptian, and a portion of them from their Babylonian bondage, for the covenant with Abraham was an everlasting covenant. And when they return from among the Gentiles, it will be their last return, their final restoration; " *to look* " (after a brief season of unequalled tribulation) *"upon him whom they pierced"*; to acknowledge him as their king; to repent and be forgiven; and to become *a blessing to all the nations of the earth*, which latter provision of the Abrahamic covenant has never, in the past, been, in any sense, or for the briefest period, fulfilled. Then will the " times of the Gentiles be fulfilled," and Antichrist and his hosts be miraculously destroyed, and his golden capital be destroyed, and down-trodden Israel be uplifted, and their beloved city become " a name of joy, and a praise and honor, in all the earth." Then will all the blessings, *both material and spiritual*, of the Abrahamic covenant, for the first time, and for all coming time, be realized by Israel, and its *spiritual* blessings by all other nations of the earth.

Such is the covenant, which God made with the fathers of Israel, with Abraham and Isaac and Jacob, commencing with a homeless but trusting and believing wanderer amidst the oaks of Moreh, and ending only when the last of his seed shall have closed their earthly career, and time shall be succeeded by the eternal state. Such, so actual, so almost inconceivable, is to be the future glory of Israel. But we need not envy her, for, when restored and pardoned, she will dispense the spiritual blessings of the covenant with overflowing fulness, with a God-like beneficence, with no invidious hand, and all other people, and kindreds and tongues will be welcome partakers of her glory. "The Gentiles shall come to thy light, and kings to the brightness of thy rising."

Every covenant hath its *seal*. The seal of the Abrahamic covenant was the rite of circumcision. Circumcision was instituted as a token of an everlasting covenant, which it was also called. "This is my covenant which ye shall keep, between me and you, and thy seed after thee: every man child among you shall be circumcised; and it shall be a token of the covenant betwixt me and you: He that is born in thy house, and he that is bought with thy money, must needs be circumcised; and my covenant shall be in your flesh for an everlasting covenant."—Genesis xvii. 6, 8.

The children of Israel might have entered into full and quiet and uninterrupted possession of their covenanted inheritance at once, and into the enjoyment of its covenanted blessings, so unconditioned, so unmingled, so glorious, but their uncircumcised hearts turned away from the God of their fathers, and they chose other and false gods, until, at last, to punish them for their sins, to bring them to repentance, to subdue their hearts and cleanse them from their iniquities, God sent them into captivity to the kings of Egypt; if so be they might thereby be made worthy heirs and possessors of so precious a heritage.

When, at the end of four hundred years, the bitterness of their bondage had become almost insupportable, God " brought them up out of Egypt"; but scarcely had they recrossed its borders, on their way to the Promised land, amidst miraculous displays of divine mercy in their behalf, when they again rebelled, and forfeited again the blessings of the covenant.

Whereupon God instituted a new covenant, entering into covenant with them, as he had entered into covenant with their fathers. But the covenant with them was not, like the former covenant, a covenant of unmingled blessing, but presented to their choice an alternative of blessing or of cursing. If they chose its curses (which they did), the Abrahamic covenant was to be, thereafter, not superseded or annulled, but *suspended*, until the covenant with them, exhausted of its curses and its coming woes, should, upon their final repentance, ensuing upon the persecutions of Antichrist, and supernatural interpositions in their behalf, be remitted and annulled by the "new and everlasting covenant of grace."

But, though suspended, how wholly unforgotten of God was his covenant with Abraham; how for ever sure its promises and its ratifying oaths! for upon the very day that God commanded them, "To-morrow, turn ye, get ye into the wilderness," he also said, remembering his covenant with their fathers, and "swearing by himself, as he could not swear by a greater," "As truly as I live, all the earth shall be filled with the glory of the Lord."

The covenant thus entered into with his rebellious children, amidst the thunders of Sinai, was the Mosaic covenant, the covenant of the Law, of the ten commandments.

If its offered blessings were accepted (as accepted they were not), the blessings of the Abrahamic covenant, both *material* (so far as themselves were concerned) and *spiritual* (so far as both themselves and, through them, "all the nations of the earth" were concerned) might begin to be realized at once, and their full consummation be speedily attained. But if the offered curse should be their choice (as their choice it was), then would the blessings of the Abrahamic covenant remain abeyant, and be realized by their children's children only, in remotest generations, after centuries upon centuries of bitterest persecution and most fiery trial had passed away. And its *spiritual* blessings, according to the proper sense and full import of its terms (as is so convincingly attested by the whole subsequent history of God's providence, and as the "sure word of prophecy" so abundantly confirms) were not " to be realized by *all other* nations and *all other* families of the earth (*through their agency*), until its blessings (both material and spiritual) were first realized by them.

We should note carefully the terms in which the Mosaic covenant is expressed. We quote but in part.

" And it shall come to pass, if thou shalt hearken diligently unto the voice of the Lord thy God, to observe and do all his commandments which I command thee this day, that the Lord thy God will set thee on high above all nations of the earth : and all these blessings shall come on thee, and overtake thee, if thou shalt hearken unto the voice of the Lord thy God, Blessed shalt thou be in the city, and blessed shalt thou be in the field. Blessed shall be the fruit of thy body, and the fruit of thy ground, and the fruit of thy cattle, and the increase of thy kine, and the flocks of thy sheep. Blessed shall be thy basket and thy store. Blessed shalt thou be when thou comest in, and blessed shalt thou be when thou goest out. . . . . The Lord shall command the blessing upon thee in thy storehouses, and in all that thou settest thine hand unto ; and he shall bless thee in the land which the Lord thy God giveth thee.

" But it shall come to pass, if thou wilt not hearken unto the voice of the Lord thy God, to observe to do all his commandments and his statutes which I command thee this day ; that all these curses shall come upon thee and overtake thee ; cursed shalt thou be in the city, and cursed shalt thou be in the field. Cursed shall be thy basket and thy store. Cursed shall be the fruit of thy body, and the fruit of thy land, the increase of thy kine, and the flocks of thy sheep. Cursed shalt thou be when thou comest in, and cursed shalt thou be when thou goest out. . . . . . and the heaven that is over thy head shall be brass, and the earth that is under thee shall be iron . . . and thou shalt become an astonishment, a proverb, and a byword among all the nations whither the Lord shall lead thee."

"I call heaven and earth to record against thee this day, that I have set before you life and death, blessing and cursing; therefore choose life, that thou mayest dwell in the land which the Lord sware unto thy fathers, to *Abraham, to Isaac, and to Jacob, to give them.*"—Deut. xxviii, xxx.

But observe how ever-mindful was God of his covenant with their fathers. Standing, as it were, upon the sure foundation of its everlasting promises, and appealing unto them therefrom, his mercy thus invites them.

"And it shall come to pass when all these things are come upon thee, the blessing and the curse which I have set before thee, and thou shalt call them to mind, among all the nations among whom the Lord thy God hath driven thee, and shalt return unto the Lord thy God, and shalt obey his voice according to all that I command thee this day, thou and thy children, with all thy heart, and with all thy soul; that then the Lord thy God will turn thy captivity, and have compassion upon thee, and will return and *gather thee from all the nations, whither the Lord thy God hath scattered thee.* If any of thine be driven into the outmost parts of heaven, from thence will the Lord thy God gather thee, and from thence will he fetch thee: and the Lord thy God will *bring thee into the land which thy fathers possessed, and thou shalt possess it; and he will do thee good and multiply thee above thy fathers."*—Deut. xxx.

" If they shall confess their iniquity, and the iniquity of their fathers, with their trespasses which they trespassed against me, and also that they have walked contrary unto me; and that I also have walked contrary unto them, and have brought them into the land of their enemies; if then their uncircumcised hearts be humbled, and they then accept of the punishment of their iniquity: Then *will I remember my covenant with Jacob, and also my covenant with Isaac, and also my covenant with Abraham will I remember, and I will remember the land."*— Levit. xxvi. 40—42.

" When all these things are come upon thee, even in the LATTER DAYS, if thou turn to the Lord thy God, and shalt be obedient to his voice (for the Lord thy God is a merciful God) he will not forsake thee, neither destroy thee, *nor forget the covenant with thy fathers which he sware unto them."*—Deut. iv. 30, 31.

But alas! alas for them, and alas for us, children of the Gentiles, whose millennium must await their millennium, whose millennium can not commence so long as we tread them down, and our times are not fulfilled, and Antichrist hath not reigned and passed away, and the tribulation inflicted upon the Jews, as a re-gathered nation, by his persecutions, hath not ceased (for when the millennium comes at last, it will come to *all*, both Jew and Gentile, and will know no discrimination between any of the inhabitants of the earth, of whatever nation or kindred or tongue, Jew or Gentile, bond or free, in the spiritual blessings it will bestow, for the millennium is but another name for the consummation, the fruition, of the spiritual blessings of the Abrahamic covenant),—alas! we say, alas for them, and alas for us! they, the children of Israel, the chosen seed of Abraham and Isaac and Jacob, even at the foot of Sinai, despised the offered blessing, and chose the offered curse. It was little less than a second apostasy, involving, as it were, in a second fall, and a deeper ruin, not themselves only, but all the nations of the earth. The weary round of those chosen curses has been rolling over their smitten land and guilty heads ever since, — is rolling now. No seats in parliaments, or cabinets, or chairs of learning, no vaults of silver and gold, stretching, Rothschild-like, their Briarean arms across land and sea, over almost the entire circle of Gentile rule, and laying their weight no where so heavily or so securely, with, as it were, so irresistible a destiny, as upon the "Promised Land," no political encompassment of thrones, no lapse of time, no witchery of music or of song, can soothe the anguish, or lull to rest the unsleeping terrors of that chosen doom.

Notice the tenderness of David in their behalf: " Seek ye the Lord and his strength; seek his face continually. Remember his marvellous works that he hath done, his wonders, and the judgments of his mouth; O ye seed of Jacob his servant, ye children of Jacob, his chosen ones. He is the Lord our God; his judgments are in all the earth. *Be ye mindful always of his covenant*, the word which he commanded to *a thousand generations;* even the covenant which he made with Abraham, and his oath unto Isaac; and hath enjoined the same to Jacob for a law, and to Israel for *an everlasting covenant;* saying, Unto thee will *I give the land of Canaan, the lot of your inheritance;* when ye were but few, even a few, and strangers in it."—1 Chron. xvi. 11—19. Ps. cv. 4—12.

But rebellious Israel remembered not his "marvellous works, and the judgments of his mouth"; they were not "mindful always" of the covenant which he swore unto their fathers. They heeded the persuasions of mercy, as little as the warnings of wrath. And yet God 'forgot, never for a moment, his ancient covenant. His heart was always turned towards them. His hand was always stretched out still. Indeed, as if to affix a final, a more solemn, seal to the Abrahamic covenant, as if to reaffirm its perpetuity, and to renew the oaths that bound it, as if, indeed, that "everlasting covenant" would not otherwise stand for ever sure, as if to anticipate their repentance and forgiveness, and its measureless wealth of unmingled blessing, he superadded to it a supplementary covenant, the covenant with his servant David, filled, not less, with unmingled and overflowing blessing, without the shadow of a curse.

"I have made a covenant with my chosen, I have sworn unto David my servant. Thy seed will I establish for ever and build up thy throne to all generations."—Ps. lxxxix. 1—4.

"Then thou spakest in vision to thy holy One, and saidst, I have laid help on one that is mighty; I have exalted one chosen out of the people. I have found David my servant; with my holy oil have I anointed him;—with whom my hand shall be established. My faithfulness and my mercy shall be with him; and in my name shall his horn be exalted. Also, I will make him, my first-born, higher than the kings of the earth. My mercy will I keep for him for evermore, and *my covenant shall stand fast with him.* His seed also will I make to endure for ever, and his throne as the days of heaven. *I will not suffer my faithfulness to fail. My covenant will I not break, nor alter the thing that is gone out of my lips.* Once more I sware by my holiness that I will not lie unto David. His seed shall endure for ever, and his throne as the sun before me."—Ps. lxxxix. 19, 20, 24—26.

Listen to the millennial invitation of Israel to "all the nations of the earth," when this covenant with David shall have been fulfilled; when Zion shall have awaked and put on her strength and Jerusalem her beautiful garments, "Ho, every one that thirsteth, come ye to the waters, and he that hath no money; come ye, buy and eat; yea, come, buy wine and milk without money and without price; incline your ear and come unto me; hear and your soul shall live; and I will make an everlasting covenant with you, even the *sure mercies of David.*"—Isaiah iv. 1—3.

This invitation is, doubtless (in a spiritual sense) both pre-millennial and millennial. It is, without question, spiritually applicable, at all times, both before and after the second coming of Christ, to all, Jew and Gentile alike, to become partakers of the spiritual blessings of the Abrahamic covenant, to be followers of Christ, and to be numbered with the elect. But in its primary and more specially intended sense, it would seem more strictly applicable to Israel in the period of her millennial glory, when in the full enjoyment of the material, not less than spiritual, blessings of that covenant.

But in the days of the covenants and invitations and warnings which we have considered, nothing availed against the rebellious obstinacy of Israel. The appeals of the greatest of their lawgivers to the thunders of Sinai: of the most eloquent and glowing of their prophets to the millennial glories of Zion, upon the second coming of their Lord; the appeals of the mightiest of their kings (though in strains attuned to a lyre that was mightier even than his throne), when he called to their remembrance the promised blessings of the covenant with Abraham, the " word which God commanded to a thousand generations," invested with an added glory by the covenant made by God with himself, were all alike in vain. Never was there, never has there been, even until now, a time, when it was not true of the rebellious House of Israel, that which was spoken by Isaiah: "Hear, O heavens, give ear, O earth; for the Lord hath spoken. I have nourished and brought up children, and they have rebelled against me. The ox knoweth his owner, and the ass his master's crib: but Israel doth not know, my people doth not consider. A sinful nation, a people laden with iniquity, a seed of evildoers, children that are corrupters: they have forsaken the Lord, they have provoked the Holy One of Israel unto anger, they are gone away backward."—Isaiah i. 2—4.

And yet listen to the yearnings, not less than to the lamentations, of God over them. " When Israel was a child, then I loved him, and called my son out of Egypt. . . . I drew them with cords of a man, with bands of love, and I was to them as they that take off the yoke on their jaws, and I laid meat unto them. . . . . But my people are bent to backsliding from me: though they called them to the Most High, none at all would exalt him. How shall I give thee up, Ephraim? how shall I deliver thee, Israel? how shall I make thee as Admah? how shall I set thee as Zeboim? mine heart is turned within me, my repentings are kindled together."—Hosea xi.

Even when their Messiah came, to plead with them; to weep over them; to gather them together as a hen gathereth her chickens under her wings, that their house might no more be left unto them desolate; to enter into a new and everlasting covenant of grace with them; they derided and reviled him; they smote him; they spat upon him; they crucified him, with as little compunction as their Roman rulers would have crucified a Roman slave. But a hidden thunderbolt, red with uncommon wrath, was about to descend upon them from the stores of heaven. "His blood be on us and on our children." And, true to the self-imprecation, his blood has fallen, and this added curse has rested, and will rest, upon them, until, at last, delivered from their captivity, and regathered as a nation in unbelief, they will be smitten by Antichrist as never smitten before, and be overwhelmed by that flood of tribulation, such as never was since there was a nation, no, nor ever shall be.

But darkness abideth only for the night, and though its latest be its deepest darkness, yet "joy cometh in the morning."

When, gathered, at last, in and around their ancient and beloved capital to defend it against the assaults of Antichrist and his innumerable hosts — summoned to the "battle of the great day of God Almighty," from the ten allied realms of the prophetic earth — they behold their rejected and crucified, but now kingly Messiah, appearing, IN PROPER PERSON, in the clouds of heaven, with power and great glory, "with the armies of heaven following"; when they behold him "standing upon the

Mount of Olives," and look upon "him" ("the *same Jesus*") "whom they pierced," when they behold him, though presented to their view, as of old, in *bodily form*, yet arrayed in the celestial splendor of resurrection glory, surrounded by the sainted dead of all the ages, and by the sainted living, arrayed, in like manner with him, in their resurrection glory: surrounded, too, by all the holy angels; when the rending earth, and the darkened sun, and the moonless and starless sky, and the shaking heavens, conspire to attest the immediate appearing of the King of kings; when they behold the manifestations of divine mercy displayed in their behalf, and of divine wrath displayed against their foes, when they witness their supernatural destruction; then, then, at last, *but not till then*, will they confess their guilt, and acknowledge their king: then "there shall be a fountain opened to the house of David, and upon the inhabitants of Jerusalem, for sin and uncleanness," and "the spirit of grace and of supplication be poured upon the house of David, and upon the inhabitants of Jerusalem," and "the land shall mourn every family apart," "as one mourneth for an only son," and blessed shall they be when they mourn; for they shall be comforted. God will accept their repentance, and "will cast all their sins into the depths of the sea." Then will be repealed the dread covenant of Sinai, and a millennium of blessing and an eternity of glory succeed to a few brief and forgotten generations of guilt, and tribulation, and shame. Then will be fulfilled that blessed trinity of covenants, the covenant of Abraham, the covenant of David, and the new and everlasting covenant of grace.

The covenant of David will exalt to his now lapsed

throne a "righteous branch," which shall "execute judgment and righteousness," and reign for a thousand years; until He shall give up the kingdom unto his Father, that God may be all in all. "And when all things shall be subdued unto him, then shall the Son also himself be subject unto him that put all things under him, that God may be all in all."—1 Cor. xv. 28.

The new and everlasting covenant of grace will descend to bless, not, as now, scattered individuals only, here a Jew and a Gentile there, but, as was confirmed unto Isaac, "all the nations of the earth."

But first of all, and last of all, and comprehending all, will be established, in fulness of millennial glory, over all the land, and over all the inhabitants of the land, the covenant with Abraham, and Isaac, and Jacob.

Says Jeremiah, looking forward to the fulfilment of this covenant;

"Behold, I will bring it [Jerusalem] health and cure, and I will cure them, and will reveal unto them the abundance of peace and truth. *And I will cause the captivity of Israel and the captivity of Judah to return*, and will build them up as at the first [which certainly has never been as yet]. And it [Jerusalem] shall be to me a name of joy, a praise and an honor before all the nations of the earth, which shall hear all the good that I do unto them; and they shall fear and tremble for all the goodness and all the prosperity that I procure unto it."
—Jer. xxxiii. 6—10.

These visions of Jeremiah of the glory and blessedness of Israel and Jerusalem, consequent upon the joint return of *all* the tribes; upon their corporate unity as a restored nation, and upon the termination of the persecutions of

Antichrist, when God's consuming vengeance and their great tribulation shall reach their full; when that which is determined shall be poured upon the desolator, and the consumption shall overflow with righteousness: were uttered by Jeremiah *more than a century* after the ten tribes of Israel were carried into that captivity from which they have never to this day returned, and in which no sure trace of them has ever been discovered. Their fulfilment belongs, therefore, beyond all question, to the future.

The verses next preceding those last quoted from Jeremiah, emphasize, more especially, the *material* blessings which will ensue upon the fulfilment of the Abrahamic covenant.

"Thus saith the Lord, Again there shall be heard in this place, which ye say shall be desolate without man, and without inhabitants, and without beast, the voice of joy, and the voice of gladness, the voice of the bridegroom, and the voice of the bride, the voice of them that shall say, Praise the Lord of hosts; for the Lord is good; for his mercy endureth for ever; and of them that shall bring the sacrifice of praise unto the house of the Lord: *for I will cause to return the captivity of the land as at the first.*

"Thus saith the Lord of hosts, Again in this place, which is desolate without man and without beast, and in all the cities thereof, shall be an habitation of shepherds causing their flocks to lie down. In the cities of the mountains, in the cities of the vale, and in the cities of the south, and in the land of Benjamin, and in the places about Jerusalem, and in the cities of Judah, shall the flocks pass again under the hands of him that telleth them, saith the Lord."—Jer. xxxiii. 10—14. Surely this revelation would seem to contemplate something more than *spiritual* blessings only.

The prophet proceeds, in the succeeding verses of the same chapter, to announce the fulfilment of the Davidic covenant; the period of its fulfilment and the contemporaneousness of that period with that of the fulfilment of the covenant with Abraham.

"In those days, and at that time, will I cause the branch of righteousness to grow up unto David; and he shall execute judgment and righteousness in the land. *In those days shall Judah be saved*, and Jerusalem shall dwell safely, and this is the name wherewith she shall be called, The Lord our righteousness. . . . . If my covenant be not with day and night, and if I have not appointed the ordinances of heaven and earth; then will I cast away the seed of Jacob, and David my servant, so that I will not take any of his seed to be rulers over the seed of Abraham, Isaac, and Jacob: *for I will cause their captivity to return*, and have mercy on them."—Jeremiah xxxiii. 15, 16, 25, 26.

Observe the descending, at the same time, of the *new* and everlasting covenant of grace, and its overflowing fulness of blessing. "Behold, the days come, saith the Lord, that I will make a new covenant *with the house of Israel*, and *with the house of Judah;* not according to the covenant that I made with their fathers in the day that I took them by the hand to bring them out of the land of Egypt; which my covenant they brake, although I was an husband unto them, saith the Lord: But this shall be the covenant that I will make with the house of Israel; After those days, saith the Lord, I will put my law in their inward parts, and write it in their hearts, and will be their God and they shall be my people. And they shall teach no more every man his neighbor, and every man his brother, saying, know the Lord! for they shall all know me from the least of them unto the greatest of them, saith the Lord: for I will forgive their iniquity, and I will remember their sin no more."—Jeremiah xxxi. 31—35.

Who will venture to say that their iniquity, or the trespasses wherewith they have trespassed against the Almighty, have ever yet been forgiven, or that their sins are not remembered still? Then can this prophecy find its appointed fulfilment in the future only.

But the crowning blessing, and crowning glory of that blissful era, will be the city of Jerusalem, "the city of the Great King," the "mountain of the Lord's house," the metropolis of the millennial earth.

" The place of my throne and the place of the soles of my feet, where I will dwell in the midst of the children of Israel for ever."—Ezekiel xliii. 7.

" O thou afflicted, tossed with tempest, and not comforted, behold, I will lay thy stones with fair colors, and lay thy foundations with sapphires. And I will make thy windows of agates, and thy gates of carbuncles, and all thy borders of pleasant stones. And all thy children shall be taught of the Lord, and great shall be the peace of thy children."—Isaiah liv. 11—13.

" And thy seed shall be known among the Gentiles, and their offspring among the peoples; all that see them shall acknowledge them, that they are *the seed which the Lord hath blessed.*"—Isaiah lxi. 9.

" And all nations shall call you blessed! for ye shall be a delightsome land, saith the Lord of hosts."—Malachi iii. 12.

The king of France complacently announced to the French Chambers, on the fourth day of December, 1841, that he had concluded a connection with the king of Prussia and the queen of England, for the consolidation of the repose of the Ottoman Empire. The repose of, at least, one portion of that empire will be consolidated by no human connections, but consolidated it will be, and when consolidated, as truly as God liveth, its repose will be sweet and everlasting, for the blessed trinity of covenants is established on sure foundations, on Heaven's firm decrees.

APPENDIX.

We extract as follows, from the work of Colonel Chesney, which is entitled, " The Expedition for the survey of the Rivers Euphrates and Tigris, carried on by order of the British Government in the years 1835, 1836, and 1837, by Lieut. Colonel Chesney, R. A., F. R. S., etc., Commander of the Expedition." (Longman's, 1850.)

"The river now about to be described (*i. e.* the Euphrates) rises at no great distance from the shores of the Euxine, and in its course to the Indian Ocean, almost skirts those of the Mediterranean. . . . . The Euphrates at one time formed the principal link connecting Europe commercially with the East. Its historical celebrity has excited in its favor an interest superior to that which has been felt for any other river; and it may reasonably be expected, that when its advantages shall be fully known, and duly appreciated, it will rise to a high degree of *political* and *commercial* importance."

" In a range of more than 1780 miles from its eastern source, this river may be said to unite three great and important seas ; which, without it, would be destitute of any water communication with each other, whilst the varied productions of the intervening territory would, in a great measure, be lost to the rest of the world." Vol. I., p. 40.

"*Bir* is one of the most frequented of all the passages into Mesopotamia, and about sixteen large passage boats are kept, ... for the use of the caravans, which occasionally number 5000 camels." P. 46.

" This great river then proceeds through the Date-groves . . . . across a bare country onwards to Hillah. . . . . This Town *is built on a part of Babylon, and chiefly with materials obtained from its ruins:* it contained, in 1831, the time of my first visit, about 10,000 inhabitants, whose dwellings are principally on the right bank; the line of houses forming an obtuse angle, almost midway between the Mujellebe and the still more celebrated Birs Nimroud." P. 57.

Extracts of Letters to Colonel Chesney, from Officers sent by him to explore the capabilities of the Euphrates for Steam Navigation and Traffic.

" SIR,

" The noble and interesting river Euphrates is far too celebrated to require from me more than a fair view of the prospect it offers for establishing an economical and more rapid communication between Great Britain and her Indian possessions, than has hitherto been attained. The brilliant prospects of a new channel being opened to our enterprising mercantile world through a steam establishment on the Euphrates, ought to awaken our best energies."

(Signed) " R. F. CLEVELAND, R.N."
" Dated 17th July, 1836."

Extract of Letter from E. P. Charlwood, Esq., R. N., to Colonel Chesney. (P. 691.)

" The Arabs always evinced great eagerness to barter their provisions, and in fact everything they possessed, for our Glasgow merchandise, ... so that I am convinced considerable commerce would be carried on with great success on the river. Taking all these things into consideration, I should say it would be highly advisable to navigate this river, as being the *speediest* and most secure route between Great Britain and her Indian possessions."

Extract of Letter from James Fitzjames, Esq., R. N., to Colonel Chesney. (P. 694.)

" The advantages that would ensue from the establishment of a regular steam communication on the Euphrates, would, I am convinced, amply repay any outlay and trouble which might attend the commencement. The avidity with which the inhabitants of the different towns on the river bought our Manchester woollen goods, &c., sufficiently proves that a great opening is presented to our commerce. Aleppo, Bagdad. Basrah, and (should the Karim be navigated) Ispahan, would soon become marts for British produce, and the influence of the British name be thus increased and extended."

"Taking these things into consideration, it appears to me, that England would not have cause to regret having made the Euphrates the high road to her Indian possessions, even should it afterwards be found that letters and passengers might be conveyed with more speed by the line of the Red Sea."

"A splendid road might be made over the 100 miles which separate the Euphrates from the Mediterranean. I should think a railroad impracticable, but I think a canal might be cut. . . . . This would complete the communication by water, of England with India, by the shortest possible line."

Extract from Letter of W. Ainsworth, Esq., Surgeon and Geologist to the Expedition.

"The river Euphrates is evidently a navigable stream. I am acquainted with it . . . . from the Taurus, to its embushure in the Persian Gulf, a distance of upwards of 1,200 miles; and in that extent, there are only two real difficulties, both of which are superable, by undergoing an expense quite disproportioned to the importance of rendering efficient at all seasons of the year, and throughout so lengthened a course, the navigation of this noble river. . . . . In a commercial point of view, the close communication thus established with so great an emporium of trade as Bagdad, is of the very first importance; nor is the connexion that would be established between Basrah and Bagdad of a trifling character; but there are also on the river between Kurnah and Felujah, large towns, as Sheikhel-Shuyakh and Hillah, and powerful tribes, as the Mountefik Arabs, who have long been actuated by the spirit of commercial enterprise."

"There is, indeed, amongst almost all the tribes a cupidity that is easily aroused, and which would stir up the people to new exertion, in order to obtain comforts and luxuries with which they would then first become acquainted, and would not be slow in appreciating. The boasted frugality and indifference of the Arab, are not proof against the inventions of an improved mechanism in cutlery or fire-arms; and nowhere is there displayed a greater anxiety for gay dresses and ornaments: this taste has become almost a passion with both sexes. We have abundant evidences of the love of decorating their children, and of a desire to improve their condition."

"The advantages which are presented by the opening of the navigation of the river Euphrates, belong to the universal civilization, as well as to increase of national power. The waters of this great river flow past the habitations of four millions of human beings, amongst whom their own traditions have transmitted, the sense of a revolution to be effected by the introduction of a religion of humility, of charity, and of forbearance."

"The intellectual powers of the descendants from the most noble stocks of the human race, are not extinct in their present fallen representatives, and it would be difficult to say to what extent civilization might flourish, when revived in its most antique home."

"The national importance of this navigation, is of the most comprehensive character. All acquainted with the history of the communication of nations, which, as Montesquieu has ably pointed out, is the history of commerce, must be aware, that those circumstances which led to the annihilation of the commerce of the East, would be revolutionised by the opening now proposed to be effected; and that whilst civilization might be confidently expected to return to its almost primeval seat, it would do so under a very different aspect, and with vastly improved means, over the days of Opis and Ophir, or of Caucasium and Callinicum." "All these advantages are to be obtained by the navigation which you have entered upon, and of which you have proved the practicability." P. 697.

Dr. Layard, writing to an eminent English merchant in 1843, says, "I believe Susiana to be a province highly capable of the most varied cultivation; the soil is rich, labour cheap, the inhabitants well disposed, and the country traversed by several noble rivers: . . . . the land is highly favorable for the cultivation of *cotton*, which is now much neglected, but which might be much improved. I made many enquiries as to the growth of hemp, . .

.. and I found the country well adapted for its cultivation." P. 701.

" Notwithstanding all the existing disadvantages, boats with merchandise are continually tracking up the rivers in Mesopotamia; but the fleets going up the Tigris against the stream, from Basrah to Bagdad, consume from thirty to forty days, while a steamer would perform this distance in four days and a half." P. 705.

" Good freights are therefore secured for steamers, and a valuable opening presented for trade, since an Arab population of about *twelve millions* is to be supplied. The actual trade to Bagdad was in 1833—12,000 bales or packages, brought up the Tigris at a freight of 1*l.* per bale."

" The establishment of the navigation, would probably lead to that of English mercantile houses at all the chief places of trade on the Euphrates and other rivers and branches at the interior stations. Pp. 704, 705.

" The wheat and barley are particularly fine; nor is it very uncommon to have three successive crops of grain in some places. The gardens yield grapes in abundance, also oranges, peaches, nectarines, figs, apples, pomegranates, and other fruits. Honey, wax, manna, and gall-nuts, are exported from the more mountainous districts, where, especially eastward of Tarabusim, the finest timber is very abundant. The scenery here is at once beautiful and strikingly grand from various points of view, as the mountains are seen rising abruptly from the sea to an elevation of four or five thousand feet, their sides being covered with dense forests, composed of gigantic chesnut, beech, walnut, alder, poplar, willow, ash, maple, and box trees, with firs towards their summits, and a magnificent underwood of rhododendron, bay, and hazel, &c. .... The less elevated grounds produce cotton, hemp, tobacco, and raw silk in abundance; besides precious stones, such as the turquoise, beryl, chrystal, pearl, and ruby. Besides the more valuable metals, gold and silver, Armenia abounds in copper, lead, iron, saltpetre, sulphur, bitumen, qnarries of coal, marble, and jasper, with several mineral springs, which have been celebrated for many ages."

" The Armenians are exceedingly fond of foreign commerce and home trade, both of which are prosecuted with such success, that even the Jews are in many instances driven out of the field of competition. The Armenians have been described as *brave*, a quality however that has long passed from them. They are now a commercial and agricultural people; well clad, abundantly fed, and possessing sheep, cattle, and fine horses in abundance." Pp. 95—99.

"The exports of Mesopotamia are: wheat, barley, rice, and other grains, horses, pearls, coral, honey, dates, cotton, silk, tobacco, gall-nuts, wool, bitumen, naptha, saltpetre, salt, coarse coloured cottons, fine handkerchiefs, and other manufactures of a country enjoying advantages which which will eventually make its commerce more important than that of Egypt." P. 109.

"The numerous towns along the Euphrates, and the extensive population, partly permanent, and partly nomadic, on the banks of that river, will ultimately require several stations; but for the present, one should be at Hillah (Babylon), and another at Anah, and a third at Beles."

"Though the subject has only been considered relatively to the people in their present state, it should not be forgotten that Mesopotamia possesses as many advantages as, or perhaps more than, any other country in the world. Although greatly changed by the neglect of man, those portions which are still cultivated, as the country about Hillah (Babylon), show that the region has all the fertility ascribed to it by Herodotus, who considered its productions as equal to one-third of those furnished by all Asia. Being equal to, and in many respects even superior to Egypt with regard to its position and its capabilities, the time need not be distant when the date-groves of the Euphrates may be interspersed with flourishing towns, surrounded with fields of the finest wheat, and the most productive plantations of indigo, cotton, and sugar-cane." Vol. II., p. 603.

To these extracts, we add, as follows, from Dr. B. W. Newton.

"The following is an extract from a letter kindly sent to me by a gentleman in India. It was written upwards of twenty years ago, after a visit to the ruins of Babylon. He was, I believe, not at all aware at that time that any were expecting the restoration and future destruction of Babylon. His conviction respecting the non-fulfilment of the prophecies of Isaiah and Jeremiah were the result of his own personal observation of facts. A few verbal alterations, not affecting the sense, have been made, and I have been obliged to leave a blank in one or two places where the manuscript is illegible."

" A fair view of the prophecies against Babylon, as given in Isaiah and Jeremiah, will show that they have not yet been fully and finally accomplished. Much has been done in demonstration of judgment against her; but her last and complete ruin is yet to come. A stone was bound to a book, and cast into the Euphrates, and it was said, 'Thus shall Babylon sink, and shall not rise from the evil that I shall bring upon her.' (Jer. li. 63, 64.) This speaks clearly of one final and irrecoverable ruin; but Babylon rose again repeatedly from the ruin that at first assailed her. Keith's book on prophecy shows that she was several hundred years being brought to desolation, and that her end was not sudden, but most gradual. Cyrus took her more than 500 years before Christ: Alexander took and attempted to rebuild her 200 years after Cyrus. In that interval her walls were reduced, and she was much shorn of her power and wealth. She was finally brought to desolation by the building of Seleucia and Ctesiphon in her neighborhood by the successes of Alexander, who thereby succeeded in drawing away the inhabitants from Babylon. She did not fall once and for all—suddenly—never to rise, like a stone cast into the waters.

" It is said that they shall not take of thee 'a stone for a corner nor a stone for a foundation.' (Jer. li.) But the ruin of the buildings at Babylon has been mainly accelerated by the removal of the materials with which she was built, for the construction of other towns in the neighborhood.

" It is said that this land of Babylon shall be a desolation, without an inhabitant (Jer. li.); but there is now the modern Arab town of Hillah and two villages besides, together with several gardens and date plantations within the limits of the ruins.

"It is said that she shall 'be a land where no man dwelleth, neither doth any son of man pass thereby.' Now, besides myriads of Asiatics, many Europeans have passed thereby, and thoroughly examined the place.

"It is said that 'the Arabian shall not pitch his tent there.' (Isaiah xiii. 20.) In 1835, when I was there, I saw marks of an Arab encampment which must have halted there for several weeks. When the Arabs make a long stay in any place, they erect mud pillars breast high, and hollowed out at the top for their horses to feed from, as from a manger. The remains of these pillars I saw; they could not have formed part of the old ruins, for a heavy shower of rain would have washed them down. My attendant explained to me what they were.

"I believe then, that Babylon will be rebuilt, and rise to the splendor described in the Book of Revelation, and that she will then suddenly and finally be brought to ruin. There are facilities in that country for bringing about such prosperity in a wonderfully short time. The soil is all . . . . mould and clay, without a single stone, and productive if watered. Formerly there were canals in all directions, fed by the Tigris and Euphrates. It is only necessary to repair the banks of these to make Babylonia the most fertile land in the globe. Wealth is so easily attained, that in a few years the Pasha of Bagdad, fifty miles from Babylon, by withholding tribute from the Sultan, was enabled to have a court rivalling that of Erzeroum."

www.ingramcontent.com/pod-product-compliance
Lightning Source LLC
Chambersburg PA
CBHW020141170426
43199CB00010B/831